School Public Relations

for Student Success

School Public Relations

for Student Success

Edward H. Moore

CORWIN
A SAGE Company

For information:

Corwin
A SAGE Company
2455 Teller Road
Thousand Oaks, California 91320
(800) 233-9936
Fax: (800) 417-2466
www.corwinpress.com

SAGE India Pvt. Ltd.
B 1/I 1 Mohan Cooperative
  Industrial Area
Mathura Road, New Delhi 110 044
India

SAGE Ltd.
1 Oliver's Yard
55 City Road
London EC1Y 1SP
United Kingdom

SAGE Asia-Pacific Pte. Ltd.
33 Pekin Street #02-01
Far East Square
Singapore 048763

Printed in the United States of America.

Library of Congress Cataloging-in-Publication Data

Moore, Edward H. (Edward Hampton), 1953–
School public relations for student success / Edward H. Moore.
    p. cm.
Includes bibliographical references and index.
ISBN 978-1-4129-6567-5 (cloth)
ISBN 978-1-4129-6568-2 (pbk.)
    1. Schools—Public relations. 2. Communication in education. I. Title.

LB2847.M66 2009
659.2'9371—dc22   2009010940

This book is printed on acid-free paper.

09 10 11 12 13 10 9 8 7 6 5 4 3 2 1

Acquisitions Editor:	Arnis Burvikovs
Associate Editor:	Desirée A. Bartlett
Production Editor:	Jane Haenel
Copy Editor:	Alice Lanyk
Typesetter:	C&M Digitals (P) Ltd.
Proofreader:	Cheryl Rivard
Indexer:	Maria Sosnowski
Cover and Graphic Designer:	Karine Hovsepian

Contents

Preface

Use this resource as your personal school public relations adviser. It has been designed to work as an on-the-job public relations partner for everyone working in schools. It is a resource to be consulted again and again as you plan and implement public relations activities to support student and school success.

This guide recognizes the vital roles that school public relations efforts play in helping students achieve and schools succeed. For students and schools to thrive, parents and communities must be supportive and involved. And the engagement and understanding needed to foster such support and involvement depend on the open, two-way, ongoing communication created by effective school public relations efforts.

The book is light on theory but heavy on practical ideas. It offers hints and tips you can use right away. It focuses on specific public relations tactics that work for individual schools and programs, as well as for school systems overall.

This guide also emphasizes the public relations responsibilities held by everyone working in schools. Of course, district administrators play key roles in nurturing communication that works. But principals, program directors, teachers, office staff, bus drivers, volunteers, and others—all persons on the front lines between schools and the people they serve—are key contributors to building understanding of and support for schools. This book offers practical ideas to assist all school employees in fulfilling these individual public relations roles.

Success in public relations often requires making the right spur-of-the-moment decisions—resulting in words and actions that will affect the reputations of schools and individuals well into the future. This guide offers sensible public relations support to every person making and implementing such choices, every single day, in schools everywhere.

Acknowledgments

I 'd like to thank the many dedicated people who work tirelessly in schools everywhere. Their determined quests to engage their communities and help their students and schools succeed inspired this work. I'd also like to thank those who generously shared their time and talent, including Frank Basso, Southern Regional Manager, New Jersey Department of Education, Division of School and District Improvement; Dr. Don Bagin, Professor Emeritus, Rowan University; Rich Bagin, Executive Director, National School Public Relations Association; Cynthia E. Banach, President, Banach, Banach & Cassidy; Dr. William J. Banach, CEO, Banach, Banach & Cassidy; Dr. Suzanne FitzGerald, Professor, Rowan University; Diane Holtzman, Business Studies Instructor, The Richard Stockton College; Larry Litwin, Associate Professor, Rowan University; and John Moscatelli, Senior Vice President and COO, Anne Klein Communications Group. Finally, a special thank-you goes to Kathy Moore, whose meticulous editing and everlasting patience were indispensable throughout this project.

PUBLISHER'S ACKNOWLEDGMENTS

Corwin gratefully acknowledges the contributions of the following individuals:

Yolanda Abel, Assistant Professor
JHU/School of Education
Baltimore, MD

Patricia N. Anderson, Associate Professor
National-Louis University
Seattle, WA

Kenneth Arndt, Superintendent
Community Unit School District #300
Carpentersville, IL

About the Author

Edward H. Moore started his career as a high school journalism teacher and school public relations practitioner. In more than 25 years as an educator, journalist, and public relations counselor, Moore has written and presented extensively on school public relations issues. He is an associate professor in the College of Communication at Rowan University. He previously served as associate director of the National School Public Relations Association and managing editor of the newsletter *Communication Briefings.* Moore is an accredited member of the National School Public Relations Association and the Public Relations Society of America.

1

The High Stakes of School PR

Student Success

*T**he stakes for school public relations are enormous:* Children excel in schools when parents are involved and communities are supportive.

And what ensures the kind of participation and support essential to this student success? Solid, open, and ongoing public relations activities that support communication between schools and the communities they serve. Of course much of this communication can be channeled in the formal ways in which public relations efforts are normally delivered—newsletters, brochures, Web sites, presentations, news coverage, and so on—but these one-way communication tactics, while vital, can do only so much.

STRONG RELATIONSHIPS
SUPPORT STUDENT SUCCESS

Public relations, as its name implies, is also about relationships. As a result, personal communication, along with such organizational communication as newsletters, Web sites, or other communication tools, is an essential ingredient in the recipe for creating relationships that work for students and schools.

Good school public relations involves much more than a formal communications program. Certainly school public relations efforts will profit from the skillful direction of a public relations administrator and staff, but success results from more than creative brochures, solid publicity, and state-of-the-art Web content. Fundamentally, school public relations efforts that work need everyone. Ultimately, success depends on what others say and do about you and everyone else in your school system.

PERCEPTIONS AND REPUTATIONS MATTER

Fair or not—accurate or not—the words and deeds of everyone involved with schools create perceptions and images that influence what others think and believe about those schools. And these images and beliefs work to promote or to discourage the kind of individual and community support and involvement essential to student and school success.

In short, all individuals involved with a school district office or school building play vital public relations roles that strengthen or damage our reputations daily. Superintendents and other district administrators may see their school districts as a collection of schools and the great programs they offer. Principals and teachers may see their schools as buildings, classrooms, busy hallways, and festive bulletin boards. But to those outside the system, these images can easily be interpreted in very different ways.

- A visitor confronted by doors locked for safety reasons may see a cold and unfriendly facade—rather than a secure learning environment.
- Someone wandering a school hallway lined with classrooms of chattering children may see disorder and chaos—rather than group learning.
- A parent offered a hasty greeting by a busy teacher may see a rude person—rather than a stressed and harried person who, in fact, is quite cordial and eager to partner with parents.

How others see and interpret everything done and said by those in schools fosters the reputations by which schools succeed or fail.

So why do schools seem to have so much trouble when it comes to public relations? The problem seems to have plagued schools and educators for a very long time. Consider the advice offered by the so-called father of modern public relations, Edward Bernays, writing more than 80 years ago:

Education is not securing its proper share of public interest. . . . The public is not cognizant of the real value of education, and does not realize that education as a social force is not receiving the kind of attention it has the right to expect in a democracy.

To explain this dilemma, Bernays continued,

> There are a number of reasons for this condition. First of all, there is the fact that the educator has been trained to stimulate the thought of individual students in his classroom, but has not been trained as an educator at large of the public.
>
> In a democracy an educator should, in addition to his academic duties, bear definite and wholesome relation to the general public. This public does not come within the immediate scope of his academic duties. But in a sense he depends upon it for his living.[1]

Just as Bernays admonished nearly a century ago, everyone involved in education, in the interest of good public relations, needs also to fulfill a role as an "educator at large to the public."

SCHOOL PR EFFORTS REFLECT REALITY

All school systems should organize and support formal public relations efforts to plan, implement, and assess communication efforts at the district and school levels, as well as in special campaigns that will need to be addressed from time to time. However, formal public relations efforts alone, while vital, simply can't ensure overall public relations success.

First, there always will be the question of competition for resources in school systems. No matter how great the need, schools will always face challenges when trying to fully fund their formal communication efforts.

Consider the numbers: By some estimates, there are about 16,000 public school systems in the United States. But only about 2,000 of these systems have administrators or others with public relations roles who are members of the National School Public Relations Association.

Does this mean that fewer than 15 percent of the school systems in the United States have formal public relations programs? Probably not. Some districts have programs that are overseen by administrators assigned public relations as one of many collateral duties. Others have some public relations programming that is overseen on a part-time basis by a teacher or perhaps a communication consultant. But the figures do dramatize the lack of formal, dedicated communications programming in many school systems, and they further highlight the importance of all individual educators making the most of their communication roles.

Second, there is the fact that a public relations program can only reflect reality. Long-term success depends on honesty and transparency in communication. Public relations isn't about papering over problems or putting a good "spin" on a bad situation. While hype and promotion might net some short-term gain, it will not create the long-term trust and goodwill essential to school success. This doesn't mean school staff members and others shouldn't tell others about the good things happening in their schools. They most certainly should. But schools shouldn't use public relations tactics to try to convince others that something is good when it is not. All communication should be honest, authentic, and true.

SCHOOL PR BASICS: DO AND TELL

There is an axiom among public relations practitioners that defines public relations as no more complicated than *doing good and getting credit for it*. Implicit in those words is the fact that public relations plays a role in making sure institutions *do* good things and *tell* others about them.

School systems have public relations—whether or not they have a formal public relations program to guide them. In any school system, day in and day out, with or without formal efforts, there are communications. Information flows. Rumors circulate. Images form. Opinions gel. And friends—or opponents—emerge.

Working together as a public relations team, those involved with schools on a daily basis (including parents, volunteers, business partners, students, school employees, and more) can be potent forces for building a better understanding of local schools and their strengths and needs. Personal communication—coupled with an overarching, institutional public relations effort—creates the ideal mix for long-term public relations success in today's schools.

Questions for Assessing School PR Support for Student Success

1. How do my public relations activities demonstrate a commitment to clear and open communication? Do I (and others) model a commitment to excellence in communication and public relations? Can I (and others) articulate the links between good communication and student and school success?

2. Do others involved with my school or program understand their specific public relations roles? How can performance in their public relations roles be monitored and measured?

3. How are others important to my efforts trained and supported to succeed in their personal public relations roles?

4. How do I help put others at ease when engaging in public relations efforts to support two-way communication? That is, how do my efforts help others to listen and speak—to offer and collect feedback as well as disseminate information and ideas? How do my public relations activities process and report on feedback in ways that show that my school or program is listening and engaged?

5. How do I access the school system's formal communication program to support and enhance my public relations effectiveness?

NOTE

1. Edward L. Bernays, *Propaganda* (New York: Horace Liveright Publishing, 1928), 121–122.

2

Understanding How PR Serves Your Students and Schools

E ducators are communicators in many ways. In public relations, the educator's "students" become the public at large. This "public classroom" environment is far less structured than the traditional one, and the "public classroom" needs a different kind of care and management.

CONNECTING TEACHING AND SCHOOL PR

Experienced teachers often counsel that two-way communication is an essential component of successful instruction in a classroom. Good teachers talk and listen. They ask questions to probe understanding and challenge thinking. They watch body language to determine student interest and involvement. They encourage interaction to foster group learning and reinforce key concepts. Similar two-way exchanges also characterize successful public relations efforts serving school districts, individual schools, and individual teachers.

In short, public relations tactics that work ensure the kind of involvement and engagement essential to school and student success. *Consider:* Public relations involves more than the dissemination of news and information. Collecting, evaluating, and acting on feedback and insights are integral parts of the process. This two-way communication exchange—actively listening as well as talking—helps build an environment of accountability, transparency, and ownership essential to building trust and credibility. This will foster the understanding and support needed for student and school success.

SCHOOL PR IN ACTION

Many school districts and school boards have policies to guide communication throughout their systems. Such guidelines can offer important direction to administrators and teachers as they fulfill the public relations roles inherent in their day-to-day instructional and administrative tasks.

However, policies alone will not ensure excellence in public relations. To work, an organization must support and commit to a program for managing its public relations efforts. It must also support and develop the skills of the people addressing the daily public relations demands. Formal public relations programs coordinate and support communication activities at all levels throughout the school system (see Box 2.1).

BOX 2.1

Example: PR Tactics in a Typical School System

Communication Methods

Forsyth County Schools, Cummings, Georgia, uses numerous methods of communication to reach stakeholders, as listed below.

School Level

Parent/teacher conferences, other face-to-face meetings

ParentPortal (online grade book, attendance, and assignments)

Infinite Campus (automated phone and e-mail messages)

E-mail and phone for all staff

PTA/O meetings

School and teacher newsletters

School and teacher Web sites

Local media

Blackboard online

School signs

Surveys

Blogs

Podcasts

District Level

Face-to-face meetings with staff

System and department Web sites (Includes "Contact Us" service)

E-mail and phone for all staff

Local media and chamber of commerce

Electronic newsletters (*The Communicator, Board Briefs,* and *Dome Digest*)

Videos (shown on www.cumminghome.com and TV Forsyth: Comcast Channel 23)

Surveys

> Soliciting feedback prior to decision making on topics such as superintendent search, tax and bond referendums, school calendar, standard-based grading and reporting, high school improvement, curriculum adoption, and counseling services.

Meetings with key communicators

Monthly on-hold recordings

ParentPortal (online)

Infinite Campus (automated phone and e-mail messages)

Print publications

24-hr. phone comment line

Informational community presentations

Customer comment feedback forms in central office foyer

Fall and spring community bus tours

Annual business after hours at new schools

Alumni directory (hardbound and online network)

Blogs

Podcasts

Community bulletin board (TV Forsyth: Comcast Channel 23)

Strategic plan (Vision 2010)

Board of Education

Face-to-face meetings

Monthly board of education meetings

Public participation

E-mail and phone

Online board agendas and supporting documents

Board meetings aired on TV Forsyth (Comcast Channel 23)

(Continued)

(Continued)

Electronic newsletter (*Board Briefs*)

Online feedback on proposed board policies

Public hearings on proposed millage rate

Local media

Community listening meetings on district wide issues (redistricting, superintendent search)

Meetings with local legislative delegation

Podcasts of monthly meetings

SOURCE: Forsyth County Schools. *Communication Methods.* Retrieved March 2, 2008, from www.forsyth.k12.ga.us/12941061621320903/blank/browse.asp?a=383&BMDRN=2000&BCOB =0&c=78713&12941061621320903Nav=|&NodeID=1873. Reprinted with permission.

Communication success relies on school employee commitment to communication excellence. In particular, district, building, and program administrators need to live up to the expected standards in all their day-to-day activities and decision making.

Typically, school public relations activities supporting communication excellence stress:

- A commitment to ongoing, honest communications to meet the information needs of all internal and external stakeholders. This includes a systematic approach to two-way communication, ensuring that leadership understands what its key audiences want and need to know and how the audiences' interests and priorities relate to key school issues and decisions.
- Decision-making guidance on issues of public information, as well as privacy, that serves the ethical and legal considerations of all key constituencies. This might include guidelines covering the release of information about students and staff. Increasingly, such rules might also speak to special challenges related to online communication by the district, its staff, and its students.

SERVING ALL SCHOOL PR AUDIENCES

Successful school public relations activities at all levels should work to ensure that the communication needs of all key audiences are addressed. These obviously include parents, students, and employees, but key audiences extend beyond those directly linked to schools and include all stakeholders essential to school and student success, for example, taxpayers, seniors, nonparent residents, new residents, area business executives and owners, political officials, religious leaders, social service agencies, law enforcement agencies, the news media, and more.

Questions for Assessing Commitments to School PR Excellence

1. How do my public relations activities support the kind of open, honest, and ongoing communication essential to student and school success?

2. How comfortable are those in my key audiences when dealing with me and my school or program? Are we perceived as warm and welcoming or aloof and standoffish?

3. How comfortable are other school or program staff members when they engage with key audience members? Are their efforts generally practical and deliberate or unthinking and reactive?

4. What specific public relations outputs can be assessed to track and improve the efforts supporting my school or program?

5. What activities in my public relations plans support individuals in fostering meaningful two-way communication?

3

Defining Your School PR Needs

I t's often easy to get people to agree that good public relations is important. Getting commitments for the resources and time needed to make it work usually is more difficult. But such commitments are critical, and they must reflect a belief that the school system's success depends on developing and supporting public relations roles in all levels of the organization.

DEFINING SCHOOL PUBLIC RELATIONS

One initial challenge involves defining just what is meant by the phrase "school public relations." *Public relations* often is used as a catchall term to describe a variety of communication and administrative endeavors, including media relations and publicity; crisis communication; meetings and special events; video, audio, and Web programming; publications; community relations; partnerships and fundraising; promotion and marketing; and so on.

While tactics may vary, the intent remains the same: Public relations seeks to build consensus and support between an organization and its stakeholders. This purpose is reflected in an "Official Statement on Public Relations" adopted by the Public Relations Society of America in 1982 (www.prsa.org), which reads in part, "Public relations helps our complex, pluralistic society to reach decisions and function more effectively by contributing to mutual understanding among groups and institutions."

The National School Public Relations Association (www.nspra.org) also underscores the commitment to building understanding and trust in its official code of ethics, by urging school officials to be "guided constantly by pursuit of the public interest through truth, accuracy, good taste and fairness."

ORGANIZING SCHOOL PR EFFORTS

Clearly, any school system should support some level of public relations programming that serves overall district needs. Many large school systems support a public relations staff, guided by a plan, that works daily to develop and deliver communication strategies and tactics to meet the district's goals and objectives.

Even smaller school systems that lack such dedicated staffing often have some form of a public relations program. It might be overseen by a part-time administrator or an outside public relations consultant. However limited, these programs still represent a commitment to communication that serves students and schools.

DIFFERENT NEEDS, DIFFERENT ROLES IN SCHOOL PR

Public relations planning should serve more than a school system's overall strategic and communication needs. Ideally, comprehensive planning and programming achieves success in three key areas:

Reaching Wide Audiences

District public relations activities reach wide audiences and support the school system's overall missions and initiatives. Usually, such efforts are proactive and assertively work to meet stated district strategic and public relations goals. They often use a wide variety of tactics, such as print, electronic, and digital communication tactics. They tend to also have strong media relations components—understandable, given the high-profile nature of school systems and their decision makers in most news media markets. They should be systematic, meaning they are plan driven and guided by both planning and monitoring research. They may be overseen by one or more public relations professionals, but they counsel administrators and others throughout the system to help them make the most of their communication roles.

Reaching Specific Constituencies

Building- and program-level public relations activities reach specific constituencies who have a stake in those buildings or programs. Building- and program-level public relations efforts might not be as formally planned as district programming, but that in no way should be taken as a sign that their importance is any less. These grassroots efforts often are the source of important linkages and relationships that are essential to district success. They put a "face" on the school system for many people and, as such, play critical roles in shaping perceptions about the system overall. Generally overseen by a principal or program administrator, these programs often rely on more traditional public relations methods, such as flyers, newsletters, local newspaper publicity, word of mouth, school Web pages, meetings, and special events.

Linking Teachers and Parents

Classroom public relations efforts link teachers and parents and create the kind of understanding and partnerships that will ensure both teacher and student success. Perhaps public relations success is nowhere more important than between the classroom and the home. Students and teachers need engaged and supportive parents to ensure academic success, but the communication environment between teachers and parents is incredibly complex. The communication needs to be constant. It needs to be characterized by transparency. It needs to be clear and concise, direct but tactful, thorough but efficient. It needs to accommodate both what the *teacher wants* to communicate and what *parents want* to know. It is both general (covering what the class overall is engaged with) and specific (offering personal communication to a parent or guardian about his or her child).

Teachers also have audiences besides parents. They're expected to communicate well with principals and other administrators; visitors, volunteers, and other community representatives; and other teachers and school professionals. New technology is adding some exciting options to the teacher's public relations arsenal, but many traditional tools continue to work well. Typically, classroom-to-home communications are characterized by newsletters and personal letters, e-mail messages, notes on homework, visits (such as back-to-school nights), phone calls, and electronic grade books and other online spaces, including classroom Web pages, blogs, and listservs.

USE AVAILABLE SCHOOL PR SUPPORT

Some school systems have a sophisticated public relations plan that addresses districtwide needs and, to varying degrees, may offer support and training for building- and program-level efforts as well as communication between teachers and parents. Administrators and teachers fortunate enough to work in such environments should always reach out to public relations administrators and seek ways in which the formal effort can help meet their own public relations needs.

Other school systems, however, may offer far more limited public relations support. In these environments, responsibility and authority for public relations practices may, by default, fall to principals, program directors, and other administrators and teachers—many of whom may have little or no formal training in organizational communication or public relations.

However, a lack of formal public relations programming and support is no excuse for any educator—teacher or administrator—to avoid formal communication efforts. Why? Remember that communication is happening whether or not you are managing it or attempting to drive it toward specific objectives. And there is good news: Basic public relations planning, and the research that supports it, need not be complicated, costly, or complex.

BOX 3.1

Examples: How to Find Help and Support for Your School PR Needs

Schools have a variety of ways of meeting school public relations needs. Some have developed a full public relations department, with a staff of specialists to handle various public relations functions. Others employ a single public relations practitioner to counsel other administrators and handle core public relations tasks systemwide. Some use outside agencies or consultants to handle certain public relations functions—often in a limited or specialized capacity. And some school systems have no formal public relations staffing; the responsibility for the function overall rests with a central administrator (often the superintendent), and day-to-day implementation of public relations functions falls on building principals, program administrators, and other school leaders.

For those working in a system with at least some public relations staffing, it's important to coordinate activities with those overseeing the district's efforts. Public relations staff members are in a position to support grassroots activities. They should be able to offer assistance in planning, support in the development of materials, help with generating publicity and dealing with news media, and more.

A school public relations staff should also be tuned in to events across the school system. As a result, they should be able to guide grassroots activities so they don't conflict or compete with one another for time and attention from key audiences. And they should be able to counsel school leaders and staff on how best to position messages and contents to reinforce the school system's overarching missions.

For those working in school systems with no formal public relations staff, many opportunities exist for getting public relations support. *One important first step:* Look into membership with the National School Public Relations Association (www.nspra.org) and one of its regional chapters. Although accredited membership is available only to school public relation practitioners, general membership in the organization is open to all educators. Along with publications and professional development activities, members also gain access to online resources and materials to support day-to-day school public relations activities. Membership also plugs educators into a regional and national network of others facing school public relations challenges—offering the chance to swap experiences and ideas.

Another source: Some public relations support may come from volunteers and other outsiders with some expertise and an interest in helping to improve school public relations efforts.

Some schools start by creating a small public relations advisory committee or study group. Those serving with this group can help create the vision and plans needed to guide the development of public relations efforts.

Committee members should represent those to be reached through these activities—such as teachers, support staff, students, parents, business partners, and others. Look for parents and business partners with public relations or other communications expertise who are willing to serve.

Along with getting advice and organizational help, volunteers might also be willing to function in some tactical public relations roles, helping to develop content or create tools such as newsletters, Web sites, special events, and more.

Some other possible sources of help: Local universities may be able to offer interns or part-time workers studying public relations. Practicing public relations professionals (or recent retirees or new parents with public relations experience) might have time to devote to school efforts. Current teachers or other staff members with backgrounds in public relations might be willing to volunteer or to accept part-time public relations roles as part of their jobs. *What to look for in potential helpers:* strong writing skills, solid online and print design skills, creative and idea-generating skills, and strong organizational skills.

One word of caution about public relations volunteers: While volunteers can be valuable in helping to plan and implement public relations activities, they will need careful guidance and a specific role. Since public relations activities communicate officially on behalf of a school and school system, a school administrator always needs to maintain direct control and oversight of and ultimate responsibility for any public relations–related activities by staff and volunteers.

BOX 3.2

Examples: School PR Steps When That Crisis Hits

Name any school job—principal, teacher, school receptionist, bus driver, and so on. None of the professionals in these positions probably thought that crisis public relations was in the job description when they took the job. Yet crisis issues can confront any school employee any day. And how an employee initially handles a potential crisis often makes the difference between public relations success and failure.

Rule 1: All school systems need to have crisis communication plans to guide employees when disaster strikes. The plans need to be rehearsed and updated regularly.

Rule 2: All school employees need to know how the plans work and what their individual roles and responsibilities are in a crisis.

Here are some school public relations examples for preparing and managing crises:

- Expect intense media coverage when a crisis—or even a rumor of a crisis—strikes and be prepared to deal with it. A school district should identify key

(Continued)

(Continued)

contacts who can handle media questions, and school employees should refer news media representatives to these spokespersons. Communicating early and often can help keep a minor event from mushrooming into a major public relations calamity.

- Have an internal feedback or reporting system for collecting insights and information on developing situations from a variety of school employees. Train employees on the importance of providing timely and accurate feedback to school officials. Employees need to understand the strong danger posed by participating in gossip and rumors during times of crises.
- Detail plans for reaching parents and others in the community quickly—for instance, Web sites, telephone- and text-message blasts, e-mails, and so on. School officials need to know that students and parents will be communicating with one another instantly by way of cell phones and text messages. Official school communications, as a result, need to move very quickly as well. If they don't, rumors and misinformation will spread and may even find their way into news media coverage of the event. *Bottom line:* Speed and accuracy help school officials practice proactive crisis public relations—a much stronger position than trying to react to misinformation and gossip.
- Never underestimate the potential for crisis even in minor situations. School crises can emerge on many fronts: violence and security issues, health and disease issues, environmental and weather issues, and so on. There is no formula for predicting crises, and major calamities often spring from what began as minor issues. *But one fact is clear:* Ignoring potential issues can create information vacuums that are breeding grounds for rumor and innuendo. All school employees need to be sensitive to the vital importance of accurately addressing potential crisis situations—and the role quick action plays in public relations success.

Questions for Assessing School PR Roles and Resources

1. Who are my key audiences and what do they want to hear from me on a regular basis?

2. How do my key audiences like to receive information from me? How are they comfortable communicating? When are they most available for communication?

3. What are my own personal public relations strengths and weaknesses? How does my personal communication make the most of my strengths? How do I compensate for my weaknesses?

4. How do I know that those in my audiences are both receiving and understanding the messages my communication carries?

5. What specific behavioral outcomes will I look for in my audience members to gauge the real impact of my public relations? In other words, how will I know when my public relations work is successful?

4

Organizing Your School PR Efforts

Organizing school public relations activities is essential to success—no matter what type of public relations effort you're trying to build. Teachers, principals, specialists, program administrators, and more—as well as public relations directors—should devote some effort to formalizing their public relations objectives and activities. Such planning is key to tracking progress and, eventually, meeting essential objectives. And it's important to keep in mind that school public relations planning often can be done quickly and easily and with little cost.

While a reasonable long-term goal might be to develop a comprehensive, formal public relations plan for a classroom, school, or school district, initial public relations development might get under way with a few more modest efforts. *For example:* A public relations initiative designed to boost attendance at an upcoming back-to-school night might be one place to start. A plan to accomplish this one task would most likely be built using many of the same plan components found in a more wide-ranging public relations effort. *The moral:* For those new to organizing public relations, starting small and growing might be the way to go.

DEFINING SCHOOL PR SUCCESS

All successful public relations efforts—no matter how limited or complex—share one attribute. They essentially link the current state of affairs to an ideal or preferred state.

17

Example

Suppose a school currently suffers from a lack of parental attendance at school meetings (the current state), and it would like to garner a 50 percent attendance rate from parents at these gatherings (the preferred state). Developing a public relations effort to hit that target would begin with research to specifically describe these two states. Planners would then use that intelligence to develop public relations tactics, with guiding strategies, to essentially "build a bridge" between the two states. So a public relations plan might be thought of as no more complex than identifying public relations activities that can take a school (or school program or school system) from where it is to where its leaders want it to be.

One important aspect of public relations involves understanding that communication objectives or outputs generally are better expressed in behavioral terms. In other words, to be most effective, public relations efforts should identify exactly what they want people *to do* as a result of being exposed to school communication.

While communication may include steps to both inform and influence audiences, public relations success generally revolves around how well communication influences thought and action.

Another Example

Consider again the school with a desire to boost attendance by parents at school meetings. Simply communicating to inform will likely not work—unless the only reason parents have not been showing up is that they had no idea when the meetings were being held. (They lacked basic information.) In all likelihood, parents were aware of or had been informed of these meetings. They need more motivators, however, to make the commitment to come to these meetings. Public relations planning would identify what those motivating factors might be and then design a public relations effort to deliver and reinforce those crucial messages. As a result, public relations success in this scenario will be more properly measured by counting heads at the meeting—measuring the behavioral impact of the communication efforts.

KEY COMPONENTS FOR SUCCESS

To link the current and preferred states, organized school public relations efforts progress through four steps:

1. The process begins with *research*—to uncover and define the issues that need to be tackled, the audiences that need to be influenced, and the best public relations methods of dealing with these issues and audiences.

2. With the best available research in hand, the *planning* phase can begin. All public relations efforts should be guided by written plans. Formal written plans need not be voluminous, but they should commit to words the precise and measurable objectives that communication seeks to reach. And the plan needs to at least sketch out the strategic and tactical approaches that will be deployed to meet those objectives. *Important:* Any plan should also address timing and budgets. *Reason:* Budgets and timing will always influence what can be accomplished. Public relations planners, in schools systems and elsewhere, rarely have all the time and money they would like to meet targeted objectives, so a plan needs to accommodate both of these issues—making sure that the communication efforts best use the money and the time that is available.

3. With a written plan in place, program administrators move on to the *implementation* phase. Here, they follow the road map outlined in the plan. They track progress in line with budgets and timeline and do research to see if messages are reaching key audiences and what effects those messages are having.

4. Finally, once the effort is fully executed, results need to be assessed in a final *evaluation* phase. Here, program administrators measure the extent to which the plan was carried out (on time and on budget), audiences that were influenced, and if the desired outcomes were achieved.

GETTING SCHOOL PR RESEARCH

Practical communication research plays a vital role in developing public relations throughout the entire process. The public relations development process begins with research to better define the problem to be addressed, as well as to outline the preferred state that successful communication will create. This research helps organizers state realistic objectives that identify the characteristics of the preferred state. (For more on school public relations research, see Chapter 5.)

This initial planning also focuses on helping to isolate precisely who makes up the target audiences, what messages are likely to be most effective with those audiences, and what combination of tactics (public relations activities) can best deliver these messages.

Communication research continues throughout the execution of a public relations effort. Such tracking or monitoring research should be conducted to see how well the activities are working toward meeting the stated objectives. And evaluation at the end of the program measures the level of final success—and may offer important insights on what worked and what didn't—insights that can be vital to improving future public relations.

While planning, tracking, and evaluation research can be complex in some situations, it need not always be cumbersome. Although budget and time constraints may limit the extent to which research can be developed, especially for those working with little or no formal public relations program support, the need for at least some basic intelligence gathering in all phases of the public relations effort still exists. Research comes in many forms. And public relations success results from knowing what research can deliver the data essential to identifying the effectiveness of any public relations effort. *Simply put:* A public relations planner should look for ways to answer the question "How are we doing?"

EXAMPLES: PUTTING SCHOOL PR RESEARCH TO WORK

Continue to consider the school trying to increase attendance by parents. Here are ways that research can contribute to school public relations: planning (initial research), implementation (monitoring research), and assessment (evaluation research).

Initial Research

A formal survey of parents might be impossible, but a few quick phone calls to a dozen or more might turn up some insights on behaviors and motivation that could offer some direction. Reviewing existing data on the links between parental involvement and student success might offer fodder for messages to help parents better understand their role in helping their children succeed. Looking at attendance rosters from past meetings might offer demographic or geographic clues as to who does show up and who is not showing up. If there is enough history, looking at past attendance records might offer other clues to issues influencing attendance, such as time, days of the week, season, and so on.

Monitoring Research

RSVPs, collected by phone, online, or e-mail, might be tracked. (Keep these tracking data to compare to performance in similar future efforts.) Lacking RSVPs, a few phone calls to gauge the likelihood of attendance among some prospects might offer clues to how well communications are working.

Evaluation Research

A headcount at the meeting will offer raw data on attendance. A brief survey of attendees might offer insights on what public relations efforts or messages they remember in learning about the meeting and deciding to attend.

The bottom line: A public relations effort should never be built upon what a few believe are the motivations or understandings that underpin a current situation. Some research should be considered to at least confirm any "gut feelings." And even limited, informal research will be better than doing no investigation at all.

SETTING SCHOOL PR OBJECTIVES

With the initial research in hand, the planning phase can begin. Here, writing concise and clear objectives, strategies, and tactics can be a challenge. *Tip:* Keep the writing simple. Don't get overly complex or descriptive. Good public relations planning copy simply states the plan's objectives, strategies, and tactics. Begin by stating objectives. An objective should succinctly state an outcome (in behavioral terms), establish a timetable or deadline for reaching the objective, and suggest a measure for evaluating achievement.

> *Sample:* On October 18, the number of parents attending the Fall Open House will increase to 40 percent of the total student population—double the attendance achieved in the last three Fall Open House meetings.

DECIDING STRATEGIES

With objectives written, the next step includes writing the overall strategies (again, based on the intelligence and insights garnered from the research) to guide the communication tactics that will be used to reach the objectives. Public relations strategies that work tie a plan's objectives to its activities and tactics. Good strategies articulate the messages and approaches that the program's tactics, when executed, will deliver. Strategies speak to the fundamental causes or restraints behind understanding and behavior. This is why strategies should be based on information uncovered in the planning research.

> *Sample:* Create a feeling of responsibility, making parents feel that their school involvement plays a vital role in their child's success in school.

There is considerable evidence showing that students perform better when parents are involved in their schools. The sample above might work in a situation where parents might be influenced to act by becoming more aware of these facts and, thus, develop a greater appreciation for the easy steps they can take to fulfill their obligation to be involved.

PICKING TACTICS

Every objective outlined in a plan may call for several different strategic approaches. And each of those strategies should then be linked to one or more tactics to finalize the implementation phase of any plan.

Simply defined, tactics are the public relations activities that will be used to deliver your messages—and perhaps channel feedback to you. In other words, tactics can be one-way (publicity in a local newspaper, for example). Or they can be two-way communication activities (a public meeting, for example, where a person is both presenting information and listening to or watching reactions to it).

In this phase, you should create a list of the various activities (or tactics) that will be used to implement each strategy. The list should be succinct, but it should contain enough description to display the tactics in action.

EXAMPLES: DEFINING YOUR SCHOOL PR TACTICS

School public relations should be carefully defined in writing. Doing so helps everyone involved better understand what needs to be done to meet the objectives that have been set. Descriptions of planned tactics need not be overly detailed. Here are a few examples of descriptions of typical school public relations tactics:

1. We will develop and deliver four weekly e-mail newsletters to parents from the principal with tips and tactics on how involved parents can help children succeed—including by attending events such as the planned open house.

2. We will develop a series of take-home flyers containing key open house details—stressing the ease of attending this one meeting—to be distributed to parents and others as they drop off and pick up their children at the school.

3. We will develop an "invitation from the teacher" template that all teachers can use and personalize to extend their own personal open house invitations to parents of children in their individual classes.

Remember: Each stated tactic should also include a brief description of the supporting activities needed to make it happen. *Examples:* the time elements or deadlines, persons accountable, and costs. These supporting details provide the foundation needed to outline the plan's timetable, staff responsibilities, and budget.

BOX 4.1

Examples: Events That Often Need School PR Planning

Public relations plans are often associated with overarching, ongoing communication efforts, but many events and activities can benefit from public relations planning. *Some examples:*

- Back-to-school nights and other school-based special events (to boost attendance and media coverage).
- School-year kickoff (to boost morale or strengthen commitment to teamwork).
- New-student registration (to increase on-time registration and create good first impressions).
- Special-purpose communication initiatives (to quell rumors and misinformation or to build understanding and support for specific decisions or new proposals).
- Milestones—such as retirements and graduations (to properly position the significance of such achievements, build pride, and generate appropriate publicity and other recognition).
- Enrollment initiatives (to emphasize everyone's communication role and improve customer service performance).
- New program or service introductions (to maximize news coverage and reinforce the school's or district's commitment to excellence).
- Employee orientations (to place the right focus on commitment to communication excellence and build the supportive atmosphere essential to it).

Checklist: The 12-Step School PR Planner

1. The overall mission of my public relations activity is to:

2. The current situation that I am trying to remedy can best be described as:

3. If successful, my public relations efforts will result in a preferred situation that can best be described as:

4. My key audiences are:

5. The messages I want to deliver to each audience are:

6. My specific public relations objectives (the actions or behavioral outputs I want to see) are:

7. The public relations strategies that will be used to reach these objectives are:

(Continued)

(Continued)

8. The specific public relations tactics I'll use to implement those strategies include:

9. My budget, broken out by tactic, includes:

10. My timeline for developing, implementing, and assessing this plan is:

11. I will monitor progress during implementation by:

12. I will assess final success by:

Q&A: Frank Basso Discusses How Schools Should Plan and Measure PR Efforts

Frank Basso is the southern regional manager for the New Jersey Department of Education, Division of School and District Improvement. Basso previously worked for the Pennsylvania Department of Social Services, specializing in Medicaid and Medicare law and policy. He has taught as an adjunct professor at both Atlantic County (New Jersey) Community College and Villanova University.

Q: There's an image of public relations in general that it has more to do with spin and promotions than open communication. Why should schools be wary of buying into this image—and what is an appropriate image for school public relations?

A: School districts, like many organizations, may have traditionally viewed the role of public relations as promotion and spin. They report that schools received an award, write a news release when they have to put out a fire, or take care of the district newsletter. This sometimes results in an incomplete image of a public relations professional as someone who simply generates hype and cover-ups. An appropriate image for school public relations professionals reflects the fact that they should be a part of the central-administration management and decision-making team. They are the conduit to the community. The practice of public relations is a proactive function, not a reactive one. Public relations practitioners are professionals who have their pulse on the needs of the community and are able to assist the central office in interpreting and addressing the needs of the community. They help schools and school leaders address issues central to the education of children. And they are in involved in fiduciary decision making that affects the education of the children. Of course they also serve as the district spokesperson and oversee significant internal communication duties.

Q: What are the kinds of public relations outputs those in schools should look for from public relations activities? In other words, what kind of bottom-line benefits can good public relations programming produce for schools and school systems today?

A: Aside from having a crisis communication plan and a media relations program, school districts should also have an extensive community relations program. In most communities, the schools are an essential part of the community. By having strong ties to the community, by having the community understand what the school district is trying to accomplish, and by having a working relationship with the community and community leaders, the school district becomes a partner with the community. Also, through a proactive approach, the public relations program can aid in encouraging parents to get involved in their children's education. All the research shows that the more parents are involved in the school, the better chance their children will succeed.

Also, in these times of economic strife and increasing financial burden on tax payers through property tax increases, funding is always an issue. In many states, bond referenda for capital improvements are usually approved by community votes. Tax increases to fund schools may need voter approval, too. A strong community relations program can mitigate any resistance to additional tax burdens to fund schools. This, of course, in the long run affects the bottom line as districts have a better chance of securing funding to provide quality education in a comfortable environment for the children. There is a direct relationship between property values and the quality of education in the community. In addition, a strong community relations program forms partnerships with local businesses and industries. Local businesses and colleges may supply school districts with space to hold meetings, with professional resources, and in the case of retailers, with supplies to assist families in need or sponsor special programs.

Q: Not all school systems are large enough to have a full-time public relations professional on staff. Should these school systems go without public relations efforts— or are there other options they can consider for public relations support?

A: No school district, regardless of the size, should go without public relations efforts. Even if the district does not have a public relations person, the district should have basic public relations plans, such as a crisis communications plan, a relationship with local media, and instruments to disseminate information to internal and external publics. Superintendents, too, must be cognizant of the importance of public relations. They must learn to develop plans and procedures to deal with these functions. School and district leaders, using a distributed leadership model, must assign these responsibilities to individuals or committees. Superintendents may need professional development in public relations functions and their effectiveness in order to monitor these efforts in the district. It is important to note that public relations efforts should not go by the wayside. Establishing a public relations program, training key personnel to assume these duties, and managing the implementation of the program are critical to effective communication to internal and external publics.

Q: School systems sometimes decide to invest in public relations after they have had problems communicating with external audiences—parents and taxpayers especially. But what should public relations also accomplish with important internal audiences— especially employees?

A: In most school districts, many members of the staff are community residents. Therefore, these people are both internal and external audiences. By having a comprehensive internal communication program that keeps the internal audience informed about what the district is doing and its goals and objectives, you satisfy the communication process to the external audience as well. The internal audience acts as key communicators, taking the message of the district and informing the external publics. The positive messages increase the credit-ability of the school district in the community and the relationship between the community and the school district. The district is able to communicate programs and services, such as adult education programs or English-as-a-second-language programs, offered by the district to the community. As mentioned before, this development of a sense of community may affect the bottom line, both from a fiscal and educational standpoint.

5

Getting Useful School PR Research

All public relations practitioners preach about the importance of collecting solid insights and intelligence before attempting to run any public relations effort. But this important initial and ongoing activity is often overlooked. *The reasons abound:* Some people fear that communication research may be too costly or time-consuming to implement—that money and time might be better devoted to actual communication rather than study. Others are concerned that the complexities of research can easily overwhelm those who simply want to initiate some basic public relations programming—why get bogged down in research when I already know what's needed?

EXAMPLES: SCHOOL PR
RESEARCH MYTHS TO ADDRESS

To help others appreciate the role of research in school public relations, some myths about practical communication research may need to be addressed. *Some examples:*

1. It is expensive. Practical public relations research need not be costly in terms of time or money. In fact, many insights that could be extremely valuable to school public relations efforts are probably being gathered already. They're lurking in the details: Who is calling

your schools, and what questions are they asking? Who is visiting your Web site, what drives them there, and what are they looking for? What kinds of concerns are repeatedly expressed in public and private conversations with parents and others?

2. It's complex. Practical public relations research need not be overly intricate. The limited scope of applied research means that large, long-term, projectable studies often aren't needed. Many times, valuable insights or data already exist and need only be organized and analyzed.

3. It's unnecessary. Personal experience should never be a substitute for practical communication research. While personal involvement in and insights on any situation can be important, such information always needs to be both explored and expanded with some practical research. In fact, research can help sort out personal biases that actually hamper understanding and addressing a communication challenge.

EXAMPLES: SCHOOL PR RESEARCH SOURCES

Consider sources of insights and information that can be tapped with little work. Those planning school public relations efforts should take advantage of the population, demographic, and behavioral data that can easily be found in many communities. *Examples:*

- Existing school district research efforts might offer insights. Studying cases from nearby school systems can offer clues about what works and what doesn't. Analyzing news coverage of schools can suggest what people know and how they feel about key school issues.
- Informal, limited polls and other data-gathering techniques might be used to supplement insights and data drawn from existing research. Short of being formal surveys, these efforts can still offer important guidance. Whether formal or informal, these efforts still should be planned and systematic. Having a plan, and being systematic, can help school public relations planners make the most of intelligence-gathering opportunities that occur regularly in schools and school systems. Planning can help schools identify and make the most of these opportunities. *Some typical scenarios:* A spike in phone inquiries, with callers asking the same or similar questions, might be predictive of an emerging controversy. Hearing fundamental confusion expressed in parent conferences or at back-to-school night on core policies or practices that are routinely covered on Web sites and in publications might suggest that existing public relations

efforts are falling short. A drop in phone inquiries and a surge in e-mail inquiries might suggest that people are changing their preferred communication methods.

- Collecting and assessing informal observations of feedback and behavior can offer a great deal of intelligence about the need for public relations activities throughout a school building or school system. They can be both harbingers of issues on the horizon as well as indicators of how well existing communications are functioning overall in your school system. As such, they play an important "monitoring" or "tracking" role in assessing how well existing communication tactics are working.

EARLY-WARNING ROLES OF PR RESEACH

Of course, insights and intelligence gathered through informal observations also might eventually signal the need for additional in-depth and more formal data collection. Witnessed often enough, seemingly anecdotal incidents may begin to be indicative of an important trend—one worth more formal investigation.

While education research in general might be seen by some as being primarily quantitative in nature, school public relations research generally includes a mix of quantitative and qualitative efforts. In other words, throughout the planning, monitoring, and evaluating stages, school communication planners seek to both count things (quantitative research) and describe things (qualitative).

Some Typical Tactics

Practical school public relations qualitative research efforts might include focus groups, in-depth interviews, or field observations. Quantitative efforts might be phone, mail, or online surveys; Web-traffic analyses; or phone-call tracking. Some tactics, such as communication audits or case studies, might include data developed through both quantitative and qualitative methods.

Designing a Research Plan

A successful, practical public relations research plan needs a clearly defined and narrow focus. This sharp focus helps to keep the scope of the work manageable and affordable. *Consider:* The work should focus on providing the basic insights essential to meeting the stated public relations objectives. It goes after only what is needed to be understood to succeed. While it may churn up information that is "nice to know," its intent is to gather insights that public relations planners need to know to succeed.

Local school districts as well as state and area education agencies frequently have demographic and polling data that can be helpful to school public relations efforts. Such research often is collected by school public relations officials—if the school system has a formal communications planning effort. But such information also may be available through school planning or business offices or educational research offices. Data on public issues collected by government and nonprofit agencies can also be helpful in understanding trends emerging in local school systems. The following are some sources of data:

- The Roper Center (www.ropercenter.uconn.edu)
- Public Agenda (http://publicagenda.org)
- The Pew Research Center for the People and the Press (http://people-press.org)
- Pew Internet and American Life Project (www.pewinternet.org)
- The Polling Report (www.pollingreport.com)
- U.S. Census Bureau (www.census.gov)
- The National Center for Education Statistics (http://nces.ed.gov)
- State education agencies (www.ccsso.org/chief_state_school_officers/state_education_agencies/index.cfm)

To collect new data and insights, consider these strategies:

- *Focus group discussions* held with key audience representatives and led by an impartial moderator. Focus groups give schools a venue in which to explore open-ended questions about key missions, messages, events, decisions, and other communication-related issues. Focus group sessions can also be used to test messages and design new online content and video or print material (including new logos, ads, mascots, slogans, and so on). *A few typical focus group audiences are:* parents new to the school or district (to assess welcoming efforts and information dissemination), uninvolved parents (to seek new ways to engage more parents), and first-year teachers (to investigate orientation and related employee communication effectiveness at the system and school levels).
- *Detailed interviews* probe for comprehensive insights and understanding on public relations issues among members of key audiences as well as opinion leaders. These in-depth interviews are structured (working from a list of planned questions) and can run a few hours or even longer. Here are *some typical targets and possible topics:* parent leaders (on external public relations issues), principals (on internal public relations issues), parents (on school- and district-level customer service issues), and teachers (on public relations training needs).
- *Content analyses* that collect and analyze data, messages, and images from a variety of internal and external sources such as local newspapers and TV, as well as school publications and Web

sites. Tracking and analyzing TV and radio news coverage, editorials and letters to the editor, incoming phone calls, Web site traffic, blogs and other online postings, school newsletters, and other publications can offer insights on both *what* is being said and *how* people prefer to receive information. Often, these analyses will have both quantitative and qualitative characteristics. That is, they may count the number of times a school or program is mentioned in a local newspaper over the past six months, and they will attempt to assess the extent to which each message was positive, negative, or neutral.

- *Customer questions and organizational files* offer more fodder for content analysis investigation. Questions and other inquiries arriving via e-mail, traditional mail, phone calls, in-person visits, and so on can be tracked and studied to spot current or emerging concerns and assess how well other public relations tactics are working at disseminating key information. Such tracking can help define positive and negative opinions, information voids or misunderstandings on key issues, confusion over plans and policies, and so on. A school or school system's own files—including memos, school-to-home flyers and brochures, newsletters, handbooks and other publications, its Web sites, and other means of communication—can provide data on how often key messages have been introduced and reinforced. User and readership surveys should also be studied to evaluate delivery of and reaction to those messages. User and reader feedback devices should solicit insights that will let schools determine if key messages were received, understood, and acted on. The interactive nature of online media (Web sites, e-mail, and e-newsletters) makes such data collection particularly easy. However, reply cards, tear-out coupons, and phone lines accepting recorded feedback can also be used to solicit comments regarding print and other traditional media efforts.

- *Communication audits* set important benchmarks while assessing performance of current public relations efforts targeting core audiences. While audits often focus on systemwide public relations efforts, they can be used to assess activity in a single school or program. Generally, audits are conducted by an outside agency or expert who can offer external insights as well as counsel on how other schools have successfully handled similar public relations issues. (The National School Public Relations Association—www .nspra.org—offers communication audit services to schools as well as insights on how to conduct audits for its members.) A communication audit generally includes a mix of secondary and primary research such as in-depth interviews with school and community leaders, observations of school meetings and events, news and school media content analyses, focus groups with representatives from key constituencies, and surveys.

Questions for Assessing School PR Research

1. What research already exists within my school system that could be helpful in shaping my public relations plans?

2. What local, regional, and national organizations can be tapped to offer opinion and demographic insights on my audiences to bolster my public relations planning?

3. Do I have a list of ongoing feedback sources that can be regularly tracked and assessed to improve my public relations efforts? *Examples:* Incoming questions, Web site traffic, comments on publications, trends in news coverage.

4. What feedback devices are offered (or could be offered) routinely in online and traditional school media? How can I track and use that feedback?

5. What two-way communication activities do I use with key contacts and influential communications to both collect and disseminate information important to my efforts?

Q&A: Cynthia E. Banach Talks About the Importance of Communication Research to School PR Efforts

Cynthia E. Banach, a former Deputy Superintendent for a Michigan Regional Service Agency, is president of Banach, Banach & Cassidy, a Michigan-based marketing research firm. She conducts survey research, develops campaign strategy, and works on community engagement initiatives. Banach has more than 25 years' experience in educational communication and marketing.

Q: Many educators think of research as costly and complex. But does practical communication research that supports school public relations efforts always have to be expensive and time-consuming?

A: No. Communication research doesn't have to be expensive and time-consuming, especially if you think of public relations research as an investment.

Public relations research can be as simple and inexpensive as reviewing census data or tracking hits on a district Web site. Or it can be more complex and costly, such as conducting in-depth surveys or communication audits. In all cases, practical communication research tends not to be excessively expensive. And in fact, it is always an investment that pays dividends.

Of course, before committing to any communication research initiative, you should first determine what you want to know and then select the most appropriate research method to gather that information.

Educators should think of research in terms of an investment in their public relations efforts overall.

Q: Why do you think schools, which seem to be so supportive of research in other areas, often balk at funding communication research to develop and assess their public relations efforts?

A: Schools frequently balk at conducting communication research for two reasons. First, they do not have clearly defined research objectives—they don't know what they want to know. And because they can't define what they are trying to discover, they can't develop a research plan.

Second, many school leaders are not aware of the research tools available to them, or they lack the knowledge to apply the tools.

School leaders can overcome this "research block" by asking a simple question: What do we want to know? Once this question is answered, it is easy to develop research objectives. Next, school leaders need to ask, What are some ways we can discover what we want to know? Then they can determine the value the research will produce.

Q: What are the risks schools face when they avoid doing communication research—and what benefits can they expect if they do some good research?

A: Avoiding communication research tends to produce two outcomes. Both are bad.

First, avoiding research can result in communication that is not relevant. For example, most parents want to know what their children are learning, how well their children are doing in school. They may also want to know something about their children's teachers and others who work directly with their children. Yet most schools do a poor job of communicating this information—even though it is very relevant to parents. At the district level, what parents want in terms of information often is ignored in favor of newsletter articles and Web site postings about issues of interest to schools—the school budget, for example. Communication research can help to balance the mix of messages by helping schools get a better understanding of just what audiences want to know.

Second, avoiding research can lead to communications that are off target. For example, parents of third graders typically are not interested in the same things as parents of high school seniors. And those without school-age children (nonparents) probably don't care about the things that interest mothers of cheerleaders.

There is a commonsense cure for off-target communication. Ask yourself—and honestly answer—who cares about this topic? Then send the message to those who care, and don't send it to those who aren't interested.

Such research can be as simple as asking people what types of school information interest them. Then send people the information that interests them. The resulting communication will be relevant and on target.

Q: Research is often associated with surveys—and surveys are important to school public relations research. But in your experience, what other research tactics can benefit schools?

A: While surveys are an essential tool to use in a communication research program supporting public relations, there are many other items in the toolbox. In fact, a careful look will discover a research tool for every research objective. Here are some examples:

- Readability formulas (to assess the reading level of publications)
- Census data (to help school leaders understand the demographics of their community)
- Focus panels (to ask in-depth questions to targeted groups of people)
- Voter records (to assess likely turnout rates of various target audiences)
- Web site statistics (to discover how many people are accessing what types of information)

- Communication audits (to conduct a comprehensive study of communication effectiveness)
- Publication audits (to determine publication effectiveness)

There are many other tools. But no matter what research tool is used, the keys to success are to have a clear research objective and to select the right tool for the job.

When contemplating a research strategy, it is important not to overlook the obvious. School leaders can conduct some effective research without much cost by simply asking questions.

Someone once said that "What do you think?" was the second most popular question to ask. ("Do you love me?" was first.) People appreciate being asked to share their thoughts. This means a school leader can conduct ongoing, minimal-cost research by asking representative groups of people what they think.

Q: How can those interested in school public relations educate others on the importance of supporting research to track and improve school public relations efforts?

A: Of course, the straightforward way to help others understand the importance of research is to give them the facts. Clearly define your research objectives, explain how the research will be conducted, and provide people with a cost-benefit analysis of how communication research supports school public relations activities.

But we know that facts alone sometimes aren't enough to convince people. So you might offer examples.

Here's one strategy: Given that people learn more from their mistakes than their successes and given that people also learn from hearing about mistakes made by others, you might gain support for research by sharing warts-and-all case studies—especially those outlining mistakes made by others.

6

Creating Goodwill Ambassadors for Your Schools

A public relations axiom warns, "You won't have good external public relations until you have excellent internal public relations."

What this means to schools: Students, staff, and others spread facts and rumors about schools far and wide through any community. Their opinions, even when based on bad information, can often carry far more credibility among family, friends, and neighbors than words and messages from official school sources.

In a sense, students, employees, volunteers, and others in schools regularly can function as goodwill ambassadors for their schools and school systems when they deal with others outside of school. Accurately informed, well trained, and properly motivated, these unofficial emissaries can help others better understand and support schools and their programs. But ill informed and lacking the right appreciation for their communication roles, these individuals can create the kind of communication damage that will be tough to undo.

EXAMPLES: THE PEOPLE WHO MAKE OR BREAK SCHOOL PR

Success depends on committing to a strong internal public relations program—one that focuses on building relationships as well as delivering messages. Internal public relations efforts should offer programming and training for all staff members and partners who work in or can be encouraged to become involved with schools:

- All staff, administrators, and teachers, including support and professional staff, as well as retirees
- Parents
- Students
- Volunteers and other visitors
- Diverse audiences
- Seniors
- Businesses and vendors
- Community, faith, and other leaders

COMMUNICATION HAPPENS: PLANNED OR NOT

It's important to remember that communication happens whether or not it's planned and supported. And a good deal of administrative activity revolves around communication—reaching consensus, announcing decisions, boosting motivation, and so on. So a formal program of targeting engaged stakeholders shouldn't be viewed as a new area of activity or as another obligation. Rather, it should be seen as simply making the most of a communication process already under way in any school or school system.

When starting public relations from the inside out, it becomes clear that those activities typically associated with a school public relations effort—such as promoting special events, generating publicity, and sending out informative brochures—represent only a small portion of those things that make school public relations successful. When public relations programming works, it usually is based on generating solid two-way communication, creating systems that are the organizational equivalent of being both a good listener and a good speaker.

LISTENING: MAKING COMMUNICATION TWO-WAY

Administrators and teachers in particular need to be supported in their roles as good listeners or collectors of feedback. They need to make sure feedback is being collected from throughout all segments of the communication and not just friendly or familiar sources. Fortunately, a number of feedback collection activities usually are already in place in many schools. Those participating in them might need to better understand the feedback roles these activities offer. That is, sometimes those in schools need to be reminded that their roles include actively listening to people and their concerns, not simply delivering information to them.

Feedback opportunities lurk in advisory committees and other such groups. Organized programs that identify and frequently communicate to a school's or school district's "key communicators" in the community also provide feedback opportunities.

EXAMPLES: LISTENING OPPORTUNITIES IN SCHOOLS

- Many opportunities to listen and collect feedback exist in less formal communication opportunities: Inviting people in for an informal breakfast or lunch on a regular basis.
- Being active, involved, and visible at community and business service clubs and other such groups.
- Organizing a speakers' bureau for your school or district.
- Keeping track of comments made in the local news media, online discussion boards, and so on.

Listening to what's being said and debated in various venues can help school employees become more aware of both good and bad information flowing through the community and more sensitive to how ongoing communication might address what's out there.

Checklist: Getting Started With Internal School PR

Assessing the impact of public relations goes beyond looking at formal communication. Public relations are concerned with what people are doing as a result of communication, not simply communication in and of itself. So assessing public relations performance and needs should include looking at what people are doing when it comes to their schools.

1. How are people encouraged to communicate with me and take advantage of my services? Is access to people and information convenient for all of those we serve?

2. Are other staff members and I familiar with and comfortable discussing all that we offer—at the school, program, and district levels?

3. Do my public relations efforts include tracking the ways in which people can offer advice and feedback? How well am I using these options? How do I assess and use this feedback?

(Continued)

(Continued)

4. How do I know if internal and external audiences can easily find and access my school and program information and advice?

5. How are my efforts creating "fans" for my school or service? What exactly are those "fans" saying about us when they talk with others who ask about our school or service?

6. How do I and other staff members define our personal communication responsibilities when it comes to coworkers? Parents? Others in the community?

7. What training is offered on a regular basis to help me and other staff members succeed in our communication roles—to support our efforts to access and share information and provide input and ideas?

7

*Achieving School
PR Success*

Employees

While there are a number of important internal audiences for any school public relations effort, perhaps none is more essential to success than those employees on the front lines, dealing with parents and the public every day. Teachers, counselors, aides, office support personnel, custodial and maintenance staff, and others all make up the team that keeps schools running, helps students achieve, and builds the kind of image others will hold about those schools.

Morale and motivation play key roles in helping people succeed in their tasks both as individuals and as team members. Solid, ongoing, effective internal public relations plays a crucial role in building and maintaining healthy morale and spirited motivation among employees.

THE REAL POWER IN
SCHOOL PR: WHEN PEOPLE CARE

People like to feel important—they like to feel as if they and their contributions matter to someone. There is no quicker way to tell people that they don't matter than to ignore them when it comes to timely communication. Imagine the impact on staff who find out about events and decisions concerning their schools from the news media, neighbors, or on the community rumor mill. *The bottom line:* Employees want to be kept informed, and they want to participate in a communication loop that allows them the chance to offer ideas and insights as well.

When employees feel as if their contributions matter, they will *want* to make their schools better. They will better appreciate their specific role in the success of their school, and they will look for ways to help individuals and teams do better work for the students and communities they serve.

CREATING A TEAM THAT WORKS

To build a team atmosphere, all school employees need to foster and model open communication. Those new to school public relations sometimes raise concerns about such an open environment, fearing that seeking too much employee input or involvement might lead to an unmanageable avalanche of communication and result in hurt feelings if employee suggestions are ignored or rejected.

But it's important to understand there's likely to be an avalanche of communication at any given time in any school—whether or not a formal program exists. It is in the unmanaged communication environments that morale is more likely to be destroyed and people are more likely to feel disengaged from the enterprise when decisions are announced. In this world, complaints, idle gossip, and vicious rumors can combine to create a whirlwind of ill will and misinformation that even the most able school employees can calm only with difficulty.

So the first step to formalizing internal public relations with frontline staff isn't about finding the time or resources to make it happen. It is about recognizing that this area of public relations is critical to overall school success and that such communication will take place—whether or not the school acts to manage it and make the most of it.

While employees need to feel free to express their opinions and ideas, they also need to understand how those expressions are evaluated and eventually how decisions affecting them and their schools are made. A chief complaint often found in employee communication surveys in schools is not that no one seeks their input but rather that no one follows up to tell them what happened as a result of their input. Most staff members don't expect all of their ideas to be put into action, but they do expect to be kept somewhat informed as information is evaluated and decisions are made.

KNOW ALL OF THE AUDIENCES

The first step in preparing to communicate with staff is to create a list of those who make up the target audiences, typically teachers, aides, counselors, substitute teachers, office staff, security or school resource officers, library staff, maintenance and custodial workers, food services workers, bus drivers, and so on. The next step is to learn how information is exchanged with these staff members on a regular basis and what needs to be done to bolster that flow of information.

Understandably perhaps, administrators often think of written or print communications when evaluating how they communicate with employees, but this review should include personal, face-to-face communication as well. Like all other public relations options, personal communication tactics need to be carefully planned and evaluated, too, and not left to the occasional opportunistic chitchat when roaming the halls or cafeteria. *One reason:* These personal exchanges facilitate effective two-way communication and offer direct opportunities to emphasize how individuals matter when it comes to school operations and student success.

IDEAS FOR SCHOOL PR ACTIVITIES WITH EMPLOYEES

Publications

Along with the district overall, every school and educational program should have a regular publication to share important news and information with employees. It need not be fancy or slickly produced. A weekly or monthly news memo on key topics or a simple e-mail in the same spirit will do. The content should be brief and to the point, communicating a respect for the time of those receiving it, and recognizing that short, succinct copy does a better job of attracting readers. If needed, the newsletter or memo can point people who want more information to sources where they can get it. One bonus of doing these publications in an online or e-mail format obviously is that links can be included allowing people to simply "click" for more information. No matter how often you choose to publish, make sure you abide by the promises made in any publication schedule. *For example:* If a publication is monthly, it needs to appear monthly—not doing so communicates that neither the publication nor its readers are very important. (Publishing on a regular schedule creates the desired perception that the publication exists to serve its readers. A sporadic publication schedule communicates that it exists to serve only the needs of the publisher—that is, it appears only when the administration wants to communicate.)

A final tip: Don't fear more frequent publication schedules. In the long run, it may be actually easier to prepare and publish a weekly digest of news and information for staff than waiting to do a monthly or quarterly wrap-up. Remember that information in today's digital environment is a swiftly moving and perishable commodity. It may be more effective for schools to be engaged in these exchanges more rather than less frequently if you want your publication perceived as tuned in and relevant to what is going on.

Staff Meetings

Tap the full public relations power available in staff meetings of every type. Properly run, meetings should be events that staff members value and look forward to. That's often not the case, however, with meetings frequently topping the list of employees' least-favored events. To this end, meetings should only be held when they are needed. Regular meetings, held whether there is a reason or not, can quickly become perfunctory events where groaning and complaints rival the exchange of positive and useful information. All staff responsible for running meetings should be given some instruction on the value of using meetings to build good communication and morale. Meetings should begin and end on time, thus communicating respect for the time of those attending. Always have a time limit to meetings, not just a starting time. An agenda of topics, speakers, or other information should always be distributed in advance of the meeting. Presenters should be prepared and not simply read PowerPoint slides or material that has been handed out to attendees. Time should always be allotted for discussion or feedback on key topics. Mix up the time that meetings are held, allowing as many sessions as possible to be held when people are bright and alert. In many schools, mornings are an ideal time for meetings, but class schedules may interfere. Still, holding all meetings late in the day can mean people are not always the most energetic. *Moral:* Look for creative ways to schedule gatherings at different times. Mix up meeting venues—moving some meetings to parts of the schools where they aren't often held (in the library, conference areas, a classroom, and so on).

A final tip: Always make a special effort to include as many school team members as possible in meetings. Although there are times when "faculty" meetings need to be held, be careful about inviting others to events dubbed "faculty meetings." Billing events as "staff meetings" or "school meetings" can help to create a more inclusive image, and including as many staff members as possible will ensure a more complete two-way flow of information throughout the organization.

Recognize Excellence in Employee Public Relations

How employees communicate with each other and with those outside of the organization affects the quality of work performed, as well as what others think about the work being done. Good public relations begins with "common courtesy," exhibited first between coworkers and then with parents and others who visit and work with schools. Beyond modeling courtesy in communication, school leaders should seek ways to recognize outstanding public relations performed by individuals. Recognize those who go "above and beyond" in responding to problems, complaints, or other potential issues. Consider a formal recognition program to reward excellent public relations and "customer service" behavior by employees. Train staff in all forms of communication that, if misused, can create problems. These include phone skills, e-mail etiquette, greeting and dealing with visitors, and so on. Help people understand that public relations can't "paper over" problems. Public relations can only strengthen good images when they exist. It's up to everyone, with the work that they do and the ways in which they deal with others, to create that image—good or bad.

Respect the Impact of Personal Interactions and Relationships

Despite the many advances in digital and online communications over the past decade, direct face-to-face communication remains the most powerful tool in every school employee's public relations arsenal. It makes sense. After all, education is an enterprise whose success depends on the thriving interaction between a school's staff and its students. Interpersonal communications of all types are core to student success. And school staff members, therefore, need to understand and respect the tremendous impact even the smallest gesture can have. In an open, comfortable communication environment, employees are more willing to raise issues and seek solutions in a spirit of cooperation—and they are less likely to feed the school grapevine with anonymous gripes and gossip. Something as seemingly simple as a cheerful greeting offered as staff members enter the building each morning can be a powerful motivator for the day. Look for opportunities to host small, informal gatherings that can facilitate two-way communication. Informal gatherings at lunch, coffee breaks with a few staff members at a time, or other such sessions can become a regular feature of active administration for any school or program. But even impromptu discussions and chats held in the course of a normal school day need to be seen as important communication events. School employees need to practice the art of active listening and be careful to respond to specific things said by others—as an important affirmation that messages have been "heard." No matter how pressured, you should avoid the appearance of being disinterested or placing a higher priority on some other event when someone stops to chat or share a comment. Apologize for not having more time, but express personal interest in the importance of the issue the person wants to discuss. Then offer another time or venue in which the information might be shared.

A final tip: Be a proactive communicator. *One way:* Keep a list of key staff members handy and review it from time to time to see who on the list you have not spoken to personally in a while. Seek out those individuals to simply offer a personal greeting and ask how things have been going.

Communicate Respect

A little common sense and courtesy go a long way when communicating with employees. And communicating in a way that signals respect for others will create an expectation that others respond in kind. Communicating respect in public relations involves both style and substance; that is, it has as much to do with the manner in which messages are delivered and received as with the messages themselves. Sometimes in communication, style trumps substance. This is a key point—since the manner of delivery in any communication will determine how well (or even if) a key message is heard and believed. Respect often is communicated in simple ways. It's important to remember to actively thank people for both extraordinary and ordinary contributions. It can help to mix up the ways in which thanks are offered. Obviously, some thanks or congratulations should be extended at meetings or other large gatherings. But other times, personal thanks shared one-on-one can be a powerful motivator. A thank-you note, handwritten, may seem like an anachronism in today's e-mail-driven environment, but a simple, handwritten, personal note of thanks can be a weighty public relations tool. Try to avoid interrupting others or "finishing" their comments or sentences for them. Be keenly aware of what body language communicates—both your body language and that of other people. No matter how stressed you feel, it's important to look interested and involved—not tired or distracted. Proactively ask for opinions and counsel from others from time to time.

A final tip: Make sure that practices in a building foster respect for the communication needs of others. For example, avoid using school public address systems for unscheduled announcements except in urgent circumstances. Keep bulletin boards, "employee"- or "student-of-the-month"-type plaques, and displays current. Doing so communicates that this is an environment in which people care and pay attention to the little things—which means a great deal to most people.

Orient—and Reorient—in the Right Way

Most organizations offer some type of orientation for new employees, but too often it focuses on the forms and policies new staff members need to know and not enough on the public relations roles important to their success and their school's success. Whether structured systemwide or done at the building or program level, all new employees should get some basic instruction on how to find and share information, who can help or answer questions on key topics, and why their communication with others—internally and externally—is important to school and student success. But don't stop with new employees. The beginning of each new school year creates a fresh *tabula rasa* upon which to help even longtime employees reorient their communication skills and practices. Whether dealing with new or veteran employees, the opening of a new school year offers the chance to welcome people and build enthusiasm for a successful year. Personal introductions—and reintroductions—are key during this time. Make sure new and experienced staff are properly recognized and introduced—in ways supportive of building the right team environment.

A final tip: Find ways to share new information and forge new relations between staff in those few important days before the school year kicks off. Once classes start, teachers and other staff will be preoccupied in getting their academic year under way, and an overload of introductory organizational communications and meetings, no matter how important, will more likely be seen as distractions and interruptions.

Checklist: Ideas for Helping Employees Deal With Upset Customers

Sooner or later any frontline employee will have to confront an upset customer. Whether in person or on the phone, how employees react in the early stages of dealing with an angry parent or other community member can make all the difference when trying to fix whatever the problem may be.

Communication training for all employees should include some activities designed to help employees defuse emotional situations and communicate with difficult people. Often, such training includes role-playing to help employees sharpen the listening and observation skills important in these kinds of situations. The training can offer possible answers to offer and steps to take when handling complaints and criticism.

Some key suggestions for those on the front lines:

1. Let people vent. This means listening at first and being careful to not interrupt—even if some obvious misstatements are being made. There will be an opportunity to "correct the record" once the person gets his or her complaint "on the record."

2. Don't get emotional. Chances are the complainer is displaying enough emotion for everyone. To keep your own emotions or anger in check, stay detached. Don't take comments personally.

3. Once the person has stated the problem, ask questions that will help to clarify the problem. Engaging in conversation at this stage may help the person begin to calm down—and see that you are concerned and interested in helping. Be careful not to phrase questions in what may be taken as a negative or accusatory tone. Instead of asking, "Didn't anyone explain that you can't get that information until you complete the form?" consider, "I'll be happy to get that information for you as soon as we fill out this form." If needed, ask the person to restate exactly what needs to be done to remedy the problem.

(Continued)

(Continued)

4. Never leave people without some explanation of what the next steps will be. Explain exactly what you will do and what they should expect to hear or see happen next. Don't refer them elsewhere without first making sure the person or office they're being sent to is aware of the situation and will, in fact, address it. If necessary, offer an apology, if not for the situation itself, then at least for the unfortunate chain of events that led them to you. Show some empathy in any apology. "I know how frustrated I have gotten in situations such as this, and I am very sorry we haven't done a better job to resolve this for you. Now, here's what we can do to address this. . . ." A simple apology can go a long way in turning a complaining customer into a cooperative one.

5. Don't get into a shouting match no matter how loud the complainer may get. If the situation escalates to a disrespectful or offensive tone, simply state that you'd be happy to help but that you cannot continue if offensive or abusive language isn't stopped.

6. Communicate that you care by always responding to a complaint left in a voice mail as soon as possible. Be personal when replying, too. Address the person by name (his or her last name unless you know the person personally). If you receive a complaint by letter or e-mail, consider responding by phone right away. A helpful voice on the phone may be just what the person needs to hear.

8

Achieving School PR Success

Parents

For most educators, putting parents at or near the top of the key partners list should come as no epiphany. Parents obviously make up a key constituency whose understanding and support are crucial to both school and student success. The bigger question is why so many school public relations efforts fail to carefully assess just what parents want to know when it comes to school information.

Like any constituency, parents have existing frames of reference that will influence their interest in and reaction to different types of communication from schools. Think of parents like a carmaker might think of its car buyers. Car buyers are somewhat interested in information about the car company overall, but their real interest lies in how a specific car will serve their needs. Customers—and parents are customers—seek out information that applies to their specific wants and needs. For those communicating on behalf of schools, this means information needs to be carefully tailored to speak to each parent's unique interest in his or her own children.

WHAT PARENTS WANT

This issue often creates a problem of message focus for schools. And it's an understandable one. *Here's why:* Most educators have extensive training in delivering the kind of controlled communication that results in outstanding instruction. Educators have, more or less, a captive audience that needs to be "schooled" in a particular set of facts or knowledge, and they map out a set of plans to interactively lead the group to an understanding of that knowledge. Their message content is communicator focused—that is, the teacher is telling his or her class what the teacher believes students *need to know.*

Most educational administrators and teachers have little if any training in the kind of communication skills generally applied in organizational communication settings. In this world, successful messages generally result from understanding what an audience *wants to know*—and not what the communicator thinks the audience *needs to know.*

As an example, a principal may be rightly proud of a new program that is the first of its kind in the state—and the principal may think parents *need to know* about this uniqueness. Most parents, on the other hand, probably couldn't care less about this feature of the program. Rather, they *want to know* how the program is going to benefit their children specifically—how the program will help their children perform better. A successful newsletter article, Web page, or meeting presentation on this program, then, should be dominated by content that speaks to how the program serves student needs and supports student success (audience focused). It should not dwell on how the program is a first of its kind or the work of years of dedicated research or sure to be a model for other schools in the district (organization focused). Such organization-focused messages may, of course, play a role at some level in a communication—to build credibility for the program perhaps. But they are not core to attracting parent interest and helping them to focus on—and buy into—the features and benefits the program offers. These messages need to be built around audience-focused news and information.

EXAMPLE: TARGETING MESSAGES TO PARENTS

One way to begin this messaging process in a school system or individual school is to consider the perceptions schools want parents to have. In other words, how do you want parents to "see" your school or school system? Perhaps it's a secure, supportive learning environment. Or maybe it's a focus on student excellence. Whatever this overarching message is, write it down. Then make a list of the ways in which individual school activities and initiatives work to support this image in ways that are important to parents. As communications are developed, seek to create messages that speak to the parents' self-interests while supporting the overarching image the school wants to support.

Example: Schools often engage in self-laudatory communication when they are able to bring class sizes down. They congratulate teachers, boards, parents, and others for their hard work and support in helping make this happen. While many parents may agree that small classes are a good thing, they may not fully understand just why this is so (or what it really means to them and their children). As a result, communication about small class sizes—lacking the right frame of reference for many parents—may simply "go in one ear and out the other."

With proper planning, messages on issues such as this might be more effective if they pull back on the self-congratulations (organization focused) and zero in on what those smaller classes now mean for individual students (audience focused): Improved performance. Higher test scores. More orderly learning environments. Greater security for students overall. These are the images schools often want to create—and the messages that parents often relate to when it comes to their children.

Whether it's proclaiming a new program, introducing new staff, or one of scores of other such announcements schools make all the time, successful communication will help a key audience such as parents put the information in the right perspective.

ANALYZE YOUR MESSAGES

Try this: Take a look at the announcements sent home to parents over the last month or two. Analyze the messages in them. Make one list of the messages that speak directly to parent interest and a second of those messages that speak mainly to the school's or district's interests. *Then ask:* How can those organization-focused messages be recrafted to become more audience focused? *One example:*

Organization focused: District experts organize a new workshop on parent and student learning activities.

Audience focused: Learn the secrets to helping your kids learn better in this new workshop.

IDEAS FOR SCHOOL PR
ACTIVITIES WITH PARENTS

Publications

Do a soup-to-nuts assessment of all publications (including newsletters, flyers, brochures, memos, and so on) being sent to parents. Print communications, especially in the elementary grades, continue to be one of the most effective ways to reach parents. Parents, in general, are more tuned in to what is happening in the classroom, and they eagerly read information carried home by students in their backpacks and folders. This interest tends to wane as children age—as does the willingness for students to carry things given to them all the way home. So one of the first steps that should be undertaken in any communication program is assessing how effective current print efforts really are. Keep track of the kinds of questions people ask when they call or visit a school or office. Talk to people, formally and informally, about how they learn about school events and announcements. See if one or more publications are specifically mentioned by name. But don't be surprised if they report that most information is gleaned from their children directly, from other parents, or in conversations with teachers. What an assessment of publications most likely will reveal is that publications are only one of a number of overlapping sources of news and information for most parents. School and even classroom newsletters often will make the list of important information sources, but you should be careful to not make the mistake of thinking that such publications alone can serve all information needs. They are only effective when people read them and then remember the key information offered in them. And remembering key information often is the result of strategic reinforcement—that is, repeating key messages to support better recall.

A final tip: Amass all of the announcements sent home to parents over the last three or four months. Some may be surprised at how little there is; others may be overwhelmed at how much there is. Too little information or too much information both present clear communication challenges to school public relations efforts. The best way to manage information flow to parents—to make sure it meets their needs without being overwhelming—might be to develop a simple flowchart of the information that is sent out on a regular basis. Such organization can help avoid overstuffing backpacks with too much information one week while having too little in another week. The real value here is in understanding that information flow to any audience—but especially parents—is too important to be left to chance. *Remember:* Bulk doesn't mean success. Simply pointing to a huge pile of paper sent to parents is not proof of any communication success. Rather, success is measured by being able to document what parents did as a result of reading those documents.

Dive Into Online Public Relations

There can be a tendency among schools to move slowly when it comes to online public relations efforts, perhaps through concern that not everyone has access to the Internet or the technical skill to communicate well online. Actually, more and more schools are finding that online communication improves access to information for many. For one thing, the on-demand nature of online communication (meaning parents can get to information when they want to access it, not when you want to give it to them—as is the case when you distribute a print newsletter or organize a meeting) opens up parent audiences to school information at times when they may not have been available in the past. *One big opportunity* is reaching parents during the workday. With more and more parents working in jobs that give them access to computers and the Internet, schools are finding they now can reach parents at times when it was nearly impossible to reach them previously. With this access also comes a new level of expectation— especially from more Internet-savvy parents. These parents have become accustomed to more and more immediate information on demand from businesses and other organizations using the Internet to market and communicate, and they expect schools to offer the same level of timely service. Clearly, this puts added pressure on schools to meet these emerging expectations for online communication, in an environment where financial resources and technical expertise may not always be the best for making it happen. At a minimum, copies (if only PDF files) of all major school publications should be available—and easily found—online on school or district Web sites. Simple site maps or other information on the site's purpose and content should be developed to help manage parents' expectations while also guiding them quickly to available information. It's crucial that someone be given the responsibility to see that Web sites are kept up-to-date, with current contact information and copies of key publications. Nothing communicates "we don't care" more than having an annual report from last year or the year before—online while the current copy can't be found. Online information updated regularly might also include current school lunch menus, schedules of activities and special events, and key rules and policies (discipline, dress codes, security, and so on).

A final tip: Web sites increasingly are becoming important marketing tools for school districts seeking to attract and keep parents and students. Sections of the site should be designed considering parent-marketing needs. They might include information about successful programs, key accomplishments, application procedures and timetables, and so on. Remember that marketing involves more than getting people to make the right choice. Marketing also is key to helping people understand that they made the right choice. In other words, keeping existing parents happy with their choice of school is how a school communication effort builds a legion of parent fans—able and willing to share the good news about schools when talking with others throughout the community.

Make the Most of Parent Meetings

It's too easy for the annual back-to-school night to become a perfunctory night out for veteran employees, while a terrifying trial by fire for newer ones. Meanwhile, such events remain high on the list of valuable activities for many parents. *The bottom line:* Back-to-school nights and other such meetings are far too important not to get the highest level of planning and preparation from all school staff involved. For many parents, these events offer one of the few—if not the only—opportunity for them to see and meet both the people working with their children and the environment in which that work takes place. An enthusiastic, well-run event will go a long way in helping these visitors feel more comfortable about the world in which their children live during the day. Visitors to any such meetings should feel welcome the minute they enter school property. Crowded rooms with too few chairs and not enough handouts communicates disorganization and a lack of caring—not the kind of first impression any school wants to create for parents. Clear signage should direct parents to parking areas, and it should greet and direct them once they enter the building. Guides should offer a printed program for the event along with a warm welcome to the school. The administrator or teacher opening the meeting should also genuinely welcome the parents, reminding them how important they are to the success of the school and its students. Ground rules for classroom visits, if they are included in the event, should be clear and fair. All teachers, especially newer ones, should be given training and support (well before the event) to help them prepare and deliver a meaningful presentation to parents—and to be comfortable in anticipating and addressing typical questions and concerns.

Typical advice: Greet parents warmly as they enter your classroom. Always introduce yourself. Plan and rehearse your presentation for the allotted time—don't run long! Stay positive. Share accomplishments and don't dwell on shortcomings. Show enthusiasm when discussing your work and your students. Share examples that help parents to see that you care about their children.

A final tip: Meeting planners should consider the overall event as well as classroom visits when planning activities such as back-to-school nights. This means parents should be left with impressions of how the school overall and individual teachers in particular work together to support school success. Student work should be prominently displayed in the hallways as well as in individual classrooms. Handouts or other documents listing overall student success should be offered to visitors, to supplement the specific accomplishments individual teachers share. In other words, the overall event should work to show that teachers and staff work individually and as a team to benefit all students.

Train Staff to Communicate With Parents

Training with a specific emphasis on parents should be a focus of staff development activities for all employees—not just teachers. Office personnel, transportation workers, and food service staff all deal with both students and parents; what they say and do can have a profound effect on parents and others throughout the community. Training should be developed to help each of these employee groups better understand and manage their own communication roles and responsibilities. It should help them better appreciate the power that their words and actions have when dealing with important audiences, such as parents. Training could help them anticipate and handle difficult questions or situations that can occur when a parent is confused, angry, or upset. It might also review data on the kinds of things parents typically want to discuss, and offer some possible responses in these areas to help employees better handle their dealings with parents. Training also might help employees distinguish how to handle their communication in various settings, such as meetings (like open house events), parent conferences, phone calls, e-mail requests, and even chance meetings elsewhere in the community.

A final tip: While training on general communication performance issues should be offered to employees on a regular basis, certain areas, such as parent communication, are such a vital part of the process they deserve even more attention. Just as a business might go out of its way to accommodate the needs of its biggest customers, schools too should look for ways to address the special needs of its core audiences. This by no means should be seen as a reason to devalue the roles of other groups important to schools. But given the higher number of regular interactions staff members are likely to have with parents, and the obviously high level of personal and emotional commitment parents will bring to these interactions, they deserve special care and consideration.

Checklist: Engagement Idea Starters for Parents

Sound school public relations efforts can create the foundation for successful involvement of parents. *Here are a few ideas for strengthening engagement with parents:*

1. Look for ways to accommodate and welcome uninvolved parents. This might include meetings at times more convenient for those who have regular work or family obligations that conflict with evening meetings.

2. Consider organizing an education or development program for parents using school staff or other experts to talk with parents about topics of interest when it comes to schools, education, and helping children succeed.

3. Always look for ways to make parents feel welcome and valued when they contact or visit your school. Find ways to communicate the value parents add to schools—noting that significant research shows that students perform better when parents are involved. Cite such data in school publications. Put welcome messages aimed at parents in key entranceways. Create a "why parents count" page on the school Web site. Comment on why schools need parents when opening school meetings and events.

4. Meet regularly with involved parents and leaders of parent organizations. Attend their meetings to display interest. Offer advice, feedback, congratulations, and thanks when appropriate.

9

Achieving School PR Success

Students

Parents are an obvious choice as key partners for schools, but students may be less obvious. While students are certainly seen as an important part of the school community, the importance of their involvement in formal school public relations activities can easily be overlooked. Nonetheless, students are a critical target audience for successful school public relations efforts.

STUDENTS TALK, PEOPLE LISTEN

Students, after all, can have a tremendous impact on school image and support as they talk with others in the community about their firsthand experiences. Well informed and properly motivated, students can be a potent communication tool for developing understanding and support. Poorly informed and lacking proper perspective, students can quickly spread unfounded rumors and other misinformation that will confound the efforts of even the most communication-savvy schools. Along with striving for accuracy in student communication, involving students in formal school communications can help them develop a better appreciation for their roles and responsibilities as good citizens in the school community.

As with any other audience, two-way communication with students is essential. When students' comments and ideas are considered, and when it's made clear that they have an obligation to be fair and accurate when sharing information, students, too, can become important communication partners for schools and school systems.

SUPPORTING SCHOOL COMMUNICATION BY STUDENTS

While involvement in communication programming may seem more logical for students in middle and high school, there can also be benefit in involving students at all grade levels in many communication activities. *Remember:* Students often are the first witnesses consulted by those who want to know what's new and what's working in schools. Good communication programming can equip them to fulfill this "unofficial spokesperson" role successfully.

School officials should make personal discussions—talking and listening to students—a regular activity during their visits to schools and programs. Teachers, counselors, and others need to make time to carefully talk with students about school issues, and they should be careful to avoid offhand remarks or expressions of frustration that students can misinterpret as they repeat such information. When staff members can't directly address issues raised by students, they should point students to those in the school system who can address their concerns, and officials who talk with students need to seriously and constructively follow up on such matters. Staff members should consider listening a priority in all discourse on school issues with students.

Communication with students ought to go beyond conversation. Personal and group conversations are vital, of course. But formal student communication plans should include print and online efforts as well.

CELEBRATE ALL STUDENT SUCCESSES

Whatever the context, school staff should always look for opportunities to celebrate student performance and congratulate achievement. Remember that student achievement is found in many venues: in the classroom (academic performance), in the gym (athletic performance), in the community (service performance), or in the home (family service). Student recognition can take the form of personal notes of congratulations, letters to parents and others, posting names on school Web sites, message boards, bulletin boards, and so on. School officials should also look for ways in which to recognize students when making presentations to community groups and outside gatherings, as well as in school meetings and assemblies. *Tip:* When appropriate, school officials should ask students to join them at communication functions, such as meetings at senior centers or with community organizations or clubs.

IDEAS FOR SCHOOL PR ACTIVITIES WITH STUDENTS

Include Students in Communications Going to Parents and Others

Copies of publications developed for parents and other external communities should be shared with students as well. If budget or other limitations make printing such documents for all students prohibitive, consider making copies available in classrooms, libraries, cafeterias, or other reading areas. Key articles might be posted on bulletin boards or other displays. Adaptations of such articles might be broadcast with daily announcements. For example, if a parent newsletter features a school program, student announcements might reference the article and include a brief interview with one or more students involved with the program. Such reinforcement can help to create common frames of reference between students and their parents as they discuss activities under way in school. Publications and other efforts might also be adapted for distribution to students. Special Web site sections, e-newsletters, and even text messages targeted to students can be effective ways to share information that also is being communicated to parents and the community in general.

Have an Effective System for Rumor Reporting and Control

Emphasize with all audiences—especially students—that accuracy and honesty in all communication is valued and expected. All school staff must be sensitive to issues being circulated on information grapevines or rumor mills, and when warranted, official communications should be promptly instituted to address and stop the flow of any misinformation. Remember that, generally, students simply want to know the reasons behind decisions and actions. Recognize and respect this natural interest and offer the background and reasoning that went into important decisions. Generally, students will accept explanations—it's the absence of explanations that creates the greatest problems. Failing to answer student demands to know the "why" behind decisions simply gives them an opportunity to conjure up their own reasons "why." And they will—generally, creatively and forcefully. Telephone rumor hotlines or special "breaking news" sections on Web sites might be used to address such emerging issues when they do erupt. School officials might meet regularly with a representative group of students or student leaders to discuss current school issues and to assess the current state and quality of communication—and what might be done to improve it.

Find Roles for Student Involvement

Some school boards have formal programs for allowing one or more students to represent student views in some fashion. And these efforts can be an important method for forging two-way communication between students and staff throughout the system. Where appropriate, programs that involve students with principals, counselors, teachers, and others can help foster open communication while instilling better understanding of school issues and operations among students. Some parent organizations also find it helpful to involve students in their work on behalf of schools and with school staff members.

Celebrate Achievements With Students, Too

While celebrating success is a staple of communications with external audiences, student contributions and success should also be shared with other students. And these accomplishments aren't limited to test scores and grades. Community service and other volunteer activities can be sources of inspiring messages for students. Such communication helps students better identify with the community of learners in which they live. Clip newspaper and other coverage of student achievements. Post the clippings on Web sites and bulletin boards. Share copies with staff. Mail copies—with a congratulatory note—to the students and parents at home.

Collect and Assess Student Feedback on a Regular Basis

Surveys aren't just for the community. It's a good idea to collect regular feedback from students as well. A formal survey is an excellent way to collect benchmark data and later additional information to track how understanding or priorities are shifting. But even if ongoing surveys are not possible, there are other ways to get important insights from students. Use technology to offer anonymous feedback devices: call-in phone lines, online feedback forms, an ombudsman-type e-mail address. Eat lunch in the cafeteria on a regular basis with rotating groups of students to conduct informal discussions.

10

Achieving School PR Success

Volunteers and Other School Visitors

Volunteers and others who visit schools on a regular basis make up another key audience needing special attention when it comes to school public relations. Because of their frequent dealings with schools and the people who run them, others in the community often see these individuals as having inside information and insights on what's good and bad about a community's schools.

WELCOMING OUTSIDERS TO YOUR SCHOOL

How these people are greeted and treated in their regular dealings with schools will influence their feelings about those schools and help or harm the reputation of the school.

Staff training in communication should stress the importance of always making visitors feel welcome and offering help to those who may look lost or in need of assistance when entering a school or navigating through it. *The bottom line:* Being a good host is everybody's job.

FIRST IMPRESSIONS LAST

Begin by evaluating exactly what about a school or office makes it a "warm and welcoming" environment to visitors. How does the environment communicate a friendly, caring atmosphere? Who is responsible for making sure visitors are greeted promptly and handled efficiently? How do staff members treat people as they enter and leave the property? When visitors leave the school, what impression do they take with them—an image of a people place or of a faceless bureaucracy?

IDEAS FOR SCHOOL PR ACTIVITIES WITH VISITORS

Conduct a "First-Impressions" Audit

Real estate agents stress the curb appeal of homes—arguing that prospects form initial opinions about a property before they ever get out of the car. The same is true for schools and school district offices. First impressions are formed as people approach the property before they ever get out of their cars. Inspect your property with the eyes of a first-time visitor. Are the grounds appealing and well maintained? Are they free of trash, litter, and graffiti? Are visitors' parking spots available and clearly marked? Are those spots convenient to the main entrance? Is the front entrance clearly marked, and, if used, are instructions for gaining access to the building prominently posted and clearly worded? Does signage begin by "welcoming" people, before giving them rules and instructions? Once inside, is the main lobby or entranceway clean and well lit? Do additional signs welcome visitors? Are displays of student work and accomplishments prominent and clearly marked? If needed, do signs clearly direct visitors to the front office? Is someone there to verbally welcome visitors and offer instructions and help if needed? Are personalized visitor badges made available—to both welcome visitors and to identify visitors throughout the building? Is it made clear to visitors how they should exit the building? Do they need to sign out or return their badges? Do you ask them to rate their visit, with a brief questionnaire or suggestion box near the exit?

Try Some Mystery Shopping

Another way to gauge the effectiveness of visitor communication is to test the system with some trial requests for service and information. Have someone track the quality of replies and responsiveness by placing calls to district and school office phones. Leave messages or request basic information, and track how often calls are answered before going to voice mail. Are requests handled by the first person to whom the caller speaks, or, if transferred, how well is the transfer performed? Do the same with tests of basic e-mail and mail inquiries. Be sure to reward outstanding service when mystery shopping spots it. Use misfires to help fashion future communication and customer service training.

Find Ways to Let Security and Friendliness Work Together

As schools have become more and more security conscious, obviously access to school grounds and properties has grown more restrictive. But security restrictions should not be used as a convenient excuse to make school visits less welcoming to visitors. In fact, as security measures increase, schools need to find creative ways to maintain a cordial atmosphere. Consider organizing a small group of employees and parents to explore ways in which their schools might be made more welcoming to community members—while not compromising security. Senior or parent volunteers, for example, might act as guides or greeters at school events, open houses, fundraising events, or other times when large numbers of visitors will be in the building.

11

*Achieving School
PR Success*

Diverse Audiences

The powerful immigration trends of the past generation have created tremendous diversity in school systems all over the United States. And with diversity have come new public relations challenges for schools—with many schools serving students and parents speaking dozens of different languages.

DIVERSITY'S IMPACT ON SCHOOL PR

Some large school systems report great diversity. The Montgomery County (Maryland) Public School Web site reports that more than 35,000 of its students come from "families without an English language background."[1] The system uses a translation system to facilitate communication, and it offers significant amounts of online content in French, Korean, Chinese, Vietnamese, and Spanish, in addition to English. Web content offered by the Fairfax County (Virginia) Public Schools includes information (key publications, announcements, policies, menus, calendars, and so on) in Arabic, Farsi, Chinese, Vietnamese, Korean, Spanish, and Urdu, in addition to English.[2] The National Center of Education Statistics notes that many languages other than English have always been spoken in the United States, and in recent years this is increasingly the case across the country. In 1990, 32 million people over the age of five spoke a language other than English in their home, 14 percent of the total U.S. population. "By 2000 [according to 2002 U.S. Census Bureau data], that number had risen by 47 percent to nearly 47 million," making up nearly 18 percent of the total U.S. population.[3]

USE PR TO TAP DIVERSITY'S POWER

School staff members obviously need to find ways in which to deliver key information in many different languages, while remaining sensitive to culture, religion, lifestyle, and other aspects that can influence the effectiveness of communication with non-English-speaking people. *The lesson:* While many might begin by simply translating information, they always risk miscommunication by failing to fully consider the more complex information needs of so-called English-language-learner students and their families.

IDEAS FOR SCHOOL PR ACTIVITIES WITH DIVERSE POPULATIONS

Enlist Key Communicators for Building Cultural and Communication Bridges

A school district should search for people among its own staff and among volunteers—from area businesses, colleges and universities, religious organizations, health care providers, social service organizations, and such groups—with the ability and willingness to work with schools in reaching out to diverse audiences. These individuals should represent the audiences you are trying to reach. They can be helpful with assessing communication needs and expectations of diverse audiences and facilitating two-way communication with them.

Welcome and Celebrate Diversity

With diversity comes a new level of opportunity for experience and learning for an entire school system. To help school system constituents better appreciate the positive aspects of diversity in schools, a special communication effort might be launched to talk about such benefits. People should be encouraged to view issues of diversity as national or global ones—not simply as local concerns. The school system should have and promote a clear policy statement on diversity and seek to appropriately highlight its efforts to strengthen diversity in staffing throughout its schools. Parents and others from various ethnic audiences should be encouraged to be actively involved in school activities and volunteer committees and organizations. *Another suggestion:* Include an appropriately diverse representation in visuals and photographs used in district Web sites and publications. Teachers and students also can help to promote a better appreciation for issues of diversity. Food, music, or language festivals can help everyone become familiar with the customs of others. Art, writing, poetry, and photography can feature various aspects of ethnic and cultural similarities and differences. Exhibits and demonstrations—including theatrical productions, fashion shows, or art displays—can help foster appreciation for and strengthen communication on diversity issues as well.

Reach Out to Diverse Populations

Work, child care, transportation, and other issues as well as language often make it difficult for new residents in a community to attend school events and meetings. District leaders should, therefore, make a special effort to reach out and meet with such audiences on their "home turf" whenever possible. Obviously, in such meetings several translators (not just one) should be on hand to work with school staff members and to answer questions. In general, initial meetings work better when personal conversations can be held with parents in their main language. Materials to be distributed should be translated as well. If community-based meeting space is not available, consider hosting such meetings in schools, but offer and promote transportation to the event as well as on-site child care during the session. Specific outreach programs might also be organized around neighborhood, church, and community organizations working with diverse populations. However it's accomplished, you should seek and test several ways in which to reach out to families who may be timid about contacting schools directly and to develop those methods that prove to be most effective. *A final suggestion:* Make the most of online communication with diverse populations. Many new residents use online communication well. They often keep in touch with friends and family around the world through e-mail and other online communication techniques. That comfort with online communication can be tapped to help ethic groups plug into local schools. Working with volunteers or translators, consider developing special Web sections or e-newsletters for ethnic groups. Follow the example of more and more school systems by having key documents and publications translated and made available online.

Use Ethnic Media to Reach Diverse Audiences

Ethnic television stations, radio broadcasters, online communities, and newspapers should be included in all school and district media and publicity communication plans. Such organizations also might be helpful in

promoting or encouraging attendance at school events and programs targeted to special populations. They also may be willing to post direct links
on their own Web sites to foreign-language publications and information
available on school Web sites. Consider creating a community or school-
based Welcome Center or online or telephone help service for non-English-
speaking families. Such services could support communication to help
new families get the most from their schools and educational programs.
These efforts might also support families in getting children and other
family members registered for school and other programs and obtaining
information on community and district resources available to them.

NOTES

1. Retrieved May 22, 2008, from www.montgomeryschoolsmd.org/mainstory/
story.aspx?id=25372

2. Retrieved May 22, 2008, from www.fcps.edu/statis.htm

3. Retrieved May 22, 2008, from http://nces.ed.gov/programs/quarterly/
vol_6/6_3/3_4.asp

12

Achieving School PR Success

Seniors

Many school systems today face the fact that the majority group in their communities is those who have no family members in schools. Lacking a direct link to schools, these people can easily become detached from schools and fail to appreciate the important value of schools to all in the community. Often, seniors represent the largest segment of nonparents and the fastest-growing segment of the overall population in many communities.

BOOST SENIOR INVOLVEMENT

To reach seniors, school systems typically try to find ways to distribute district publications to them. Some also sponsor programs to offer free or reduced-price tickets to athletic events, plays, and other school programs. But to meaningfully engage seniors, schools need to offer more active involvement that provides an opportunity to build working relationships— the kind of relationships that will result in a higher level of understanding of and commitment to supporting school needs and initiatives.

Engaging seniors effectively means finding ways in which their expertise and needs can be matched in mutually beneficial ways to the needs and expertise of other key school audiences—such as students and staff. Successful programs often involve mentoring activities, where seniors can interact with students in reading or athletic or field trip activities. But they also should reciprocate by offering seniors support in developing computer or other technical skills, encouraging contribution to living history efforts, and so on.

Schools should develop efforts to identify those in the senior audience who would like to be involved and reach out to them with communications expressing the school system's genuine interest in having them get involved with schools.

IDEAS FOR SCHOOL PR ACTIVITIES WITH SENIORS

Link Students and Seniors in Meaningful Ways

Both in schools and in senior neighborhoods and living centers, there should be programs to find ways in which students and seniors can build relationships by sharing expertise. Such efforts are much more than "doing-good" events aimed at generating a good image. Having seniors work directly with students helps erase many of the misconceptions or bad images they may hold about today's young people. By seeing and getting to know the "products" of today's school systems, seniors are directly reminded of the importance of schools in helping young people develop and succeed. *Some involvement examples:* Student groups and volunteers might organize computing-skills, foreign-language, or photography classes for seniors. Regular presentations or exhibits might be organized for seniors, to highlight student art or theatrical work. To get seniors into schools, consider efforts to allow seniors to enroll in or audit classes with available seats. Encourage seniors to guest-lecture in classes or afterschool programs about personal interests or hobbies, their travels, or their personal experience in historic events.

Actively Recruit Seniors for Volunteer Efforts

For schools, many seniors have the golden mix of expertise and the time to share it. By welcoming them into volunteer programs, schools will benefit from their expertise immediately and in the long term as involved seniors become fans and spread goodwill for schools to others throughout the senior community. But special efforts should communicate the important ways in which seniors can contribute to school efforts and reach out specifically to invite seniors into school programs. *Some involvement examples:* Find roles for seniors in student mentoring and skill-building programs. Include senior leaders in any key communicators network. Always include seniors in any budget or finance or bond election committees. Find special programs to encourage informal visits by seniors to schools, such as allowing them to join students for lunch or breakfast in school cafeterias. Open school hallways or gyms to seniors before or after school for walking or other activity programs—and encourage students and staff to join them.

Target School Communications Directly to Seniors

Seniors generally are one audience still committed to reading print publications. But they're increasingly becoming more comfortable with online communication, especially e-mail. As a result, schools should talk with seniors about their online communication activity and consider developing e-newsletters or e-mail communication programs targeting seniors. Special sections of school Web sites also might be developed with content aimed at seniors. But traditional print communications need to reach seniors, too. Special efforts can be used to make sure school newsletters, brochures, and flyers reach them. Deliver school publications in bulk for distribution at local senior centers or communities. Have publications available at other local venues where seniors often visit, such as libraries, doctors' offices, or other medical facilities.

Q&A: Diane Holtzman Talks About Involving Seniors in School PR Efforts

Diane Holtzman's research interests include generational diversity in the workplace and in the classroom. She has written on generational diversity, the use of electronic portfolios in assessment, and service learning in marketing and management. Holtzman teaches advertising at Rowan University, and she is a business studies instructor at The Richard Stockton College.

Q: Why are seniors such an important audience for schools?

A: Our seniors are an important voting sector in local elections and know how to become organized around issues that are deemed important for their interests. This ability of seniors to organize and take action on school board issues or on initiatives for increased school budgets comes from seniors' backgrounds that were influenced by historical events such as the organized protest movements of the 1960s and the controlled classroom activities that influenced their styles in solving problems. Seniors often have well-organized clubs and senior activity groups that provide a forum to communicate their messages about school issues. In addition to being a strong voting block, often with the time and desire to vote on school issues, seniors are important consumers of services and programs that schools offer to the community. Whether seniors attend plays or musical events at the schools, or teach a noncredit course in the evening, they are consumers of the events and outreach activities provided. From this, seniors feel connected to their schools in the community. Many seniors are part of a networked community through 55+ communities or local senior citizen centers. Do not overlook including seniors in focus groups and in recognizing them as an active constituency that needs to be communicated to throughout the year, not just at times for special elections and bond votes.

Q: Do schools need to communicate with seniors differently than they do with other audiences?

A: Communicating with seniors needs to take different forms. Many seniors rely on print media as their main source of information—local newspapers can't be overlooked for sending messages about school issues and initiatives. These forms of communication work well with those seniors who have time to spend reading an entire article and have time to understand the details in the message. Since this generation of seniors is accustomed to reading as the primary form of information gathering, newsletters have a place in the communication mix. When writing for the print media and newsletters, use the active voice in sentence structure, write clear messages by using everyday language, not techno-jargon, and get to the point of the message quickly—all of these components become essential in developing the message for the seniors. Don't forget to look at the type size and typeface for your newsletter stories. Avoid using fonts that are sans serif and smaller than 11-point type.

In understanding the senior generation, do not overlook that many seniors are in a segment of the population that has trust in schools. This trust in schools as part of the seniors' belief system is based on their childhood and early adult experiences when schools were there as a positive service for the public good. Seniors trust in the messages sent by schools—so don't violate the trust of this sector by sending mixed messages on issues or distorting the true costs of initiatives. Once trust is broken with this sector, it is hard to regain their interest in reading what is disseminated.

Research also indicates that many seniors are important in rearing their grandchildren—the school messages need to be communicated to the grandparents as well as to the parents.

In addition, many seniors are savvy in the use of basic word processing programs, e-mail to communicate with friends and family, and Web sites for information. It's not unusual to visit a 55+ senior community and see the rooms with computers and Internet access crowded at all times during the day. Therefore, don't overlook providing a site on your school's Web page with information that may be of interest to seniors about programs and activities at the schools for them or for opportunities to integrate seniors into the school programming as guest lecturers or library aides.

Q: Most seniors have little or no direct connection with what happens in schools. How can schools make them care more about the success of students and schools?

A: It does not have to take many additional dollars to show a generation of seniors that schools care about their input, but it does take keeping that cohort "top of mind" when planning upcoming yearly events or programs within the classrooms. Keep in mind that this generation is connected through tight-knit communities and through strong senior organizations such as AARP. One positive experience by a senior can be exponentially spread to many others within the community. Part of our public relations outreach as school leaders is to hear the voices of all external constituencies in strategically planning how to position the school stronger within our communities. What greater story can we share with young adults than showing the value and respect we give to the voices of older generations? In the diversity of many of our schools, intergenerational sharing of family stories and the imparting of the culture is commonplace. Other schools can look to this diversity of cultures and customs regarding the incorporation of seniors into educational communities as a model to replicate.

The more we recognize the strong value of communicating positive stories about our students, such as the gains students make in both personal and academic achievements, the more the senior population begins to hear the "good" about what the schools do within the community. This requires diligence on the part of school leaders in writing and encouraging the regular coverage of positive stories. From recent demographic trends, many grandparents are now instrumental in their grandchildren's schooling—don't forget the roles these seniors play: as guardians of children using the schools for education, and as members of the community looking for programs to meet their interests as senior adults. Messages in newsletters, and on school Web sites, should recognize these dual roles for seniors today and craft stories that show what the schools offer for these discrete needs.

Last, schools can investigate the value-added benefits of forging stronger ties between groups such as Girl Scouts, Boy Scouts, Boys and Girls Clubs, and 4-H groups with senior centers in the community by encouraging them to participate in afterschool programming for children. This win-win situation of incorporating three—if not four—generations in programming for children would spread throughout the community and send a strong message to voting members of the community.

Q: Many people try to develop programs to get seniors into schools to help garner their support. Is getting seniors to visit the schools all it takes to build meaningful relationships?

A: Although getting seniors into the schools is essential for seniors to experience all that is taking place within our classrooms, it is also important for schools to reach out to the senior communities through visits to senior centers and to the clubhouses of the active adult communities or other senior living centers. Consider using speakers' bureaus sponsored by the schools. Having teachers and other school staff members—and junior/senior students—go out to the senior communities to speak about different educational topics or school issues helps build relationships.

Q: Schools sometimes avoid using the Internet and online communication to reach seniors believing they lack the skills or access needed to communicate online. Can online communication be made to work with seniors?

A: Although our seniors have many commonalities as a generation, within that cohort there are different levels of sophistication in using the online resources. Many in the senior community know how to access online sites to find information about consumer issues, check investments, or communicate with children and grandchildren. Many have used computers in their workplaces; adult children have introduced them to computers as a way to share photos and personal communication. Yet within the generation there are seniors who do not go to online resources and still rely on print media and telephone calls as their main forms of information retrieval. As school leaders, we have to recognize that one form of communication—to one homogeneous audience—no longer works in our society. We need to understand our audiences—the generations that are in our districts—and to recognize that targeting our messages to their needs is important. We also need to recognize that a printed newsletter or a news release will no longer suffice in reaching all of our seniors. Multiple communication tactics must be used to reach our seniors—including printed newsletters, speakers to groups, school Web sites, online podcasts, blogs, e-mail messages, e-newsletters, and more.

13

Achieving School PR Success

Businesses and Vendors

Businesses in the community and vendors doing business with schools and school systems are another key group to be tapped and engaged to help build a better understanding about school efforts and needs throughout the community.

TAP BUSINESS EXPERTISE AND INFLUENCE

Business leaders, because of their position in the community, can be a powerful voice for or against schools—depending on their experiences and resulting points of view. And when it comes to public relations, some business leaders may need special attention to help them fully appreciate the special circumstances schools face as they operate their organizations and make decisions.

Consider: People tend to approach any situation in the frame of reference their personal experiences have constructed. As such, some businesspeople might be tempted to first look at schools through the lens of a successful business operator—someone faced with the day-to-day challenges of building a healthy balance sheet and bottom line. Schools measure profits and progress in other ways, however. And some school procedures and policies may seem quite foreign to some businesspeople. As businesspeople and schools find ways to learn from one another, a true "win-win" situation can result. While school leaders can help business leaders better understand the unique challenges schools face, business leaders can help schools become efficient and find better ways to measure progress and performance.

BUILD WORKING PARTNERSHIPS

Typically, schools seek partnerships with area businesses to generate mentoring or internship opportunities for students. Some also seek business support for fundraising or foundation initiatives. These are solid roles in which businesses can meaningfully support schools and students. But they can become just one-way programs that, after time, make schools seem part of a long line of organizations seeking only money from businesses. Long-term, successful business involvement creates meaningful partnerships—in which genuine synergy between the groups creates value for both schools and businesses.

IDEAS FOR SCHOOL PR
ACTIVITIES WITH BUSINESSES

Make Your Schools Business Friendly

Look for ways to get business leaders into schools—making it clear from the outset that you are looking for mutually beneficial working relationships and not just handouts. Offer to host business meetings or luncheons in school facilities. Select a group of business leaders to work with top administrators as key communicators on topics important to the community in which both schools and businesses operate. Invite them to attend a meeting or luncheon at the beginning and end of the year to talk about school events and progress, and explore ways in which businesses and schools can work to support one another. Keep these leaders on school publication distribution lists so they receive key newsletters and other publications. Urge them to share important school information with other business and community organizations they're involved with. Look for special projects to do with businesses. *Example:* A speakers' bureau joint venture where school experts can run programs for local businesses, business experts can offer programs for school staff and students, and both groups can jointly sponsor programs for the community in general.

Link Students With Business Leaders

As with other key community audiences, linking students with business leaders can help dispel any misconceptions business leaders might have about students and schools—and help remind them of the important work schools and the community can do together to help students succeed. *Some possibilities:* Follow up school visits by business leaders for meetings or luncheons with brief school tours or presentations on key programs run by students. Encourage businesses to host performances or presentations by students at business meetings and special events throughout the year. Work with businesses offering high-traffic opportunities, such as shopping malls, downtown business associations, community fairs, and so on, to sponsor exhibits of student work or performances or presentations by students.

Joint Venture on Public Relations and Marketing Initiatives

Businesses often have communication and marketing programs and tactics that can be tapped to help school communications. Business communication experts might be willing to advise schools on developing their programs and improving the effectiveness of them. School-related content should be developed and made available for use in company publications (such as employee and customer newsletters) as well as on company Web sites. School information and key messages might also be used in some corporate advertising or marketing efforts. Businesses with a direct interest in school information, such as real estate agencies, might be interested in helping develop content on schools and their programs and offering links to school Web sites on their company Web sites. Publications and other materials might be made available in lobbies and waiting areas of businesses in the community. Student-made or school-focused videos might air on television monitors in waiting areas—or streamed on company Web sites.

Q&A: John Moscatelli Discusses How Schools and Businesses Can Work Together

John Moscatelli is senior vice president and chief operating officer at Anne Klein Communications Group (www.akleinpr.com), a national public relations firm based in the Philadelphia region. His responsibilities include strategic planning and counseling, client service, account supervision, and staff management. Moscatelli previously spent 15 years with Earle Palmer Brown Public Relations, Philadelphia, where he served as senior vice president and associate general manager. He has an extensive background in crisis communications, media relations, product publicity and promotion, community relations, internal communications, spokesperson training, and video production, and is an accomplished speech and scriptwriter. Moscatelli is an accredited member of the Public Relations Society of America (PRSA) and a member of PRSA's College of Fellows.

Q: Why would businesses be interested in working with or partnering with schools? What's in it for them?

A: Businesses are interested in working with schools for any number of reasons, from purely philanthropic to purely marketing. And schools can take advantage of what businesses have to offer in any number of ways. As part of the community, some business owners or managers see it as their civic duty to become involved in the schools. Others see it as an investment in the company's future, a way to ensure a supply of educated, motivated future employees. Others see strong schools as a recruitment aid, to help convince candidates for employment to relocate to a community where their children will get a terrific education. Some use participation in school activities to help season their executives, to develop their management and communications skills, to engender a sense of community involvement that reflects the company's philosophy. Some businesses see involvement as a way of building immediate business (fundraising partnerships with parent organizations, for example) or as a way to reach parents with their marketing messages (hospitals sending health information to homes via the children). Some business leaders simply see it as a way of giving back to the community that is enabling them to be in business and make a living.

Q: What are the biggest mistakes schools often make when reaching out to businesses and other organizations to seek support and partnerships?

A: There are many:

1. Not asking. You can't wait for them to volunteer. You have to ask.

2. Asking for too much. Don't expect any one business to take on an entire project. Divide the "ask" into digestible bits that businesses can act on without a huge financial commitment.

3. Forgetting that businesses have other things to do. Schools may be important, but they are not the business's only or primary interest.

4. Asking at the wrong time of the year. Find out when the businesses in your community make decisions about charitable donations. When do they put their budgets together? When should you make your request to make sure you are included in their budget? Asking after all the budgeted funds have been committed will simply elicit a negative response.

5. Not inviting the business owner or manager to be part of the planning. They may turn you down—but if they do agree, you've made a much stronger ally who can help reach into other segments of the business community.

6. Taking cooperation for granted. Don't assume they will continue to support you year after year. Things change.

7. Failing to say thank-you. And saying it in a meaningful way.

8. Not building relationships. If the first and only time the business owners or managers hear from you is when you want something from them, expect a "no" answer.

9. Not assessing your own internal connections. Who do your teachers and your active parents know? Where do their spouses work? Can you conduct an inventory of connections to see where you might have some leverage?

10. Not publicly recognizing their support. If permissible in your system, can they display banners, distribute literature or giveaways, set up an informational booth, be mentioned in the program or thanked from the podium, included in a newsletter article about the event?

11. Forgetting you are dealing with people, not "companies." People (owners, managers) will be making the decision, not the company. Frame your request in human terms and remember that emotion trumps logic almost every time.

Q: How do businesses operate differently than many schools—and why is it important for schools to understand and appreciate these differences?

A: Businesses are in business to make a profit. They cannot give it all away. Schools need to be reasonable in what they request and recognize they are competing with many other non-profit organizations for a share of philanthropy. Business executives have many time constraints, and schools need to be respectful of their time. Businesses expect to see an ROI (return on investment)—what are you offering? Businesses have mission statements and corporate philosophies. How does what you want fit in with their corporate culture? If you can draw a connection, you may have a better chance of getting what you want from them. Most businesses today operate on a just-in-time premise—just enough people and resources to get the job done on time. There's not a lot of slack in the system, so if they are going to do something to help the school, they are either giving up something important to the business or they are going to have to work extra to accomplish their business goals. You are asking them to make a sacrifice, no matter how small, and you need to recognize that. (Yes, you face many of the same, if not even tighter, restrictions on budget and staffing, but this is not the business's problem.)

Q: What, besides money, can businesses offer to schools and their students?

A: On the philanthropic level, many businesses allocate funds to worthy causes directly or through employee committees, and in some cases businesses will match donations their employees make. Smaller businesses may not be in a position to donate cash, but they may be able to provide in-kind donations (food, beverages, or promotional materials). Many local businesses, particularly fast-food operations, will offer schools and parent-teacher organizations (such as local PTA and PTO groups) the opportunity to conduct fundraisers. Other businesses might donate services (painting, plumbing, landscaping, or printing). Some businesses encourage executives and up-and-coming employees to get involved in their communities, to serve on boards and committees, to speak to students, to conduct tours and visitations, to support field trips. Some businesses may make products available for sampling or to support an event. Some may make donations for auctions.

First, figure out what you need. Then, develop a list of targets—companies that may be able to provide what you need. Then, determine if you have any relationships that can help you reach out to those companies. Then, develop the "ask." Be specific. At the same time, try to be creative, too. Don't limit yourself in your thinking. As you develop the "ask," think about the "wifm," the "what's in it for me" from the business's point of view. *Remember:* Individual people will be reviewing your request, not a company.

Q: What are some of the better ways schools might approach businesses to explore potential partnerships? Should they come looking for specific kinds of support—or would it be better to involve businesses in brainstorming the possibilities?

A: Your approach to businesses needs to be tailored to the individual businesses and to the type of support you need. The local pizza franchise may have a co-op marketing program that encourages them to partner with school parent groups for fundraisers. Another small business might provide small cash donations or in-kind services. Larger businesses might want to have their employees participate in community activities and make people available to serve on committees or boards.

One approach is to inventory the businesses in your community.

- What are they? What do they do?
- What is their track record for supporting community activities (talk to others, monitor media coverage of business philanthropy, talk to the chamber of commerce)?
- Who do you know who knows them (parents, teachers, spouses, vendors, and so on)?
- Develop a "business plan" that outlines what you'll need and a target list of which businesses you think can provide what you need.
- Find out how the businesses want to be approached (letter; e-mail; personal visit; informal interaction at a group meeting, such as a Chamber of Commerce or Lions Club meeting; phone call from someone they already know).
- Tailor the request to something that fits that company and its style or culture.
- Keep track of the requests so you know who responded and who did not and what the next steps might be.
- Where possible, get company executives involved in the brainstorming and planning to give them some sense of ownership. Make sure you share results with them so they can see if their efforts have been successful and to keep them motivated.

Q&A: Dr. William J. Banach Discusses How Marketing Can Contribute to School PR Efforts

Dr. William J. Banach is CEO of Banach, Banach & Cassidy, a Michigan-based marketing research firm. He conducts survey research, tracks societal trends, and is considered "the godfather" of school marketing.

Q: Marketing is often associated with corporate communication and selling. Why should schools also consider marketing when evaluating their public relations options?

A: The obvious reason schools should attend to marketing is that the game has changed. Schools now function in a free-market environment than enables students and parents to exercise a variety of options. In addition to the historically available choices of public, private, and parochial schools, students and parents can now choose from a list of options that also includes home schooling, corporate learning centers, charter schools, online cyberschools, and more. At the high school level, "dual enrollment" in community colleges and universities has become an option for students and parents to consider. In a competitive environment filled with learning options, school leaders disregard marketing at their own peril.

Further, many states now tie funding to enrollment. This means that school leaders have a financial incentive to market their schools and programs. As schools lose enrollment in this new "get a student, get state aid" game, they endanger their ability to provide viable programming and risk—to use the words of free-market advocates—going out of business. Quite simply, competition for available revenue has created an environment in which successful marketing is the prelude to quality school programming.

Another—and, unfortunately, less obvious—reason school leaders should market their schools and programs is that it is the right thing to do. Effective marketing programs build better public understanding. Better public understanding builds higher levels of public support. And higher levels of public support translate into enhanced educational programming.

Q: What can marketing efforts accomplish for schools?

A: Marketing can create and establish a marketplace position or identity for schools. It can help a school be known as "really good" or as the school with "the best reading program" or "the rigorous math program" or as the school "that prepares students for . . ."

By establishing a position—or identity—marketing can provide a foundation for communication that reinforces and enhances what people believe about a school.

In marketing, everything begins with beliefs. The famed media theorist Marshall McLuhan famously said that the perception *is* the reality. He was right. If people think you are good, you *are* good. And if they think you are bad, well . . .

Given the decadeslong criticism of public schools, it's nonetheless fair to say that most American schools are better than people think they are. Marketing can turn this reality into the public perception. The result can be as dramatic as watering a dry plant. Suddenly, energy is released, and the school begins to grow.

Effective marketing communication can also improve internal public relations, especially when combined with a dynamic strategic plan. It can get the entire staff "on the same page," enabling staff to leverage their communication resources by delivering a consistent public relations message. In this type of communication environment, what one person communicates can positively reinforce another person's communication, and what the two of them communicate can positively reinforce everyone else, and so forth.

Q: What are some of the key audiences schools should attempt to reach with marketing?

A: The key audiences depend, of course, on the school's marketing goals. *If the goal is to maintain or increase student enrollment, the key audiences might include:*

- Parents of newborns (convincing them that the school district is a wise choice when their child reaches school age—preferably preschool age)
- Realtors (informing and engaging realtors can extend the sales force for the school district)
- Parents of school-age children, particularly at the elementary level (to assure them that their children are receiving a quality education and to help them be testimonial givers for the school district)

If the goal is to pass a financial proposal or a bond, the key audience will be people who are most likely to vote in the next school election—as opposed to registered voters.

If the goal is to engage the community and develop a strategic plan, the key audiences might be all of those 55+ people without school-age children, members of the business community, civic leaders, and school staff. *Ask these questions to determine the key marketing audience:*

- What do we want to market?
- To whom?
- Why?

Once schools determine what they want to market, the key target audiences become apparent. And once schools articulate why they want to market to these key target audiences, their marketing goal becomes more clearly defined.

Q: Schools generally aren't known for their marketing expertise. What's the best way for them to get started with marketing?

A: Just as schools learned to improve curriculum, pass referenda, and plan strategically, they can learn to market. Those undertaking school marketing efforts can start by reading a marketing primer, attending a conference, and visiting a school that has a successful marketing program. They also can engage an outside consultant.

The first step is to understand what marketing is and is not. The second step is to define the school district's marketing goals. And the third step is to determine if the school district has the necessary expertise and financial resources.

Schools also must realize that marketing requires commitment if it is to pay dividends. While marketing activities can be initiated at the central office level, each school in the school district must support and complement the marketing initiative. Ultimately, the overall goal is to help all school employees become ambassadors—or marketing agents—for their schools and their school districts.

Q: In your experience, what are the things schools should try to avoid doing when developing efforts to market?

A: The first thing to avoid is the temptation to position the school district as "Number 1." There are about 16,000 school districts in America, and the odds are very good that your district is not the very best in the country. And even if your school district is the very best, odds are people wouldn't believe you if you told them.

This caution serves to underline again that marketing is about what happens in the heads of consumers. (It is not about what is happening in your head!) The perception is the reality! *Schools can avoid most marketing potholes by asking these questions:*

- Is what I am saying true?
- Is what I am saying easy to understand?
- Is what I am saying believable?

In the end, nothing beats open, honest communication. Marketing is no different.

14

Achieving School PR Success

Community Leaders

Active leaders in civic associations, faith organizations, and other service groups offer another avenue for collecting and disseminating information important to school and student success.

ENCOURAGE ACTIVE INVOLVEMENT

One of the most important strategies for building working relationships is to encourage administrators and other staff to be actively involved in these organizations. This means more than just joining—it includes attending meetings regularly, serving on committees, volunteering for special projects, and other expressions of commitment. Demonstrating commitment to an organization is an important first step in generating similar commitments to support schools and school programs.

Faith community members in particular can be underused resources. Since these leaders frequently deal with the same social and family issues as schools, they are in a unique position to help build programs and initiatives that serve both school and community needs. Through their congregations, faith leaders also are in a position, when properly informed, to share information on school services and programs with wide audiences throughout the community.

IDEAS FOR SCHOOL PR ACTIVITIES WITH COMMUNITY LEADERS

Target Public Relations and Involvement Programs to Faith Communities

Leaders in the religious communities frequently express strong interest in learning more about school programs and services. Their positions and interests often overlap directly in school interests in addressing many community and family needs. A group of key communicators among faith leaders might be created to meet periodically with school administrators to explore areas of common interest and support. Schools might develop information on their programs for community and other organizations to use in their publications and Web sites. Faith leaders and their organizations can be helpful in establishing direct connections with ethnic audiences important to a school's diversity-communication efforts as well.

Encourage School Involvement by Elected and Government Officials

Elected officials and others who work in government have an obvious interest in understanding school operations and being fluent in discussions of school programs and success. Be sure to include economic development officials in these activities. Their interests in promoting local and regional benefits often directly tie to school initiatives and needs and can also help students and staff. *Some suggestions:* Sponsor visitation programs for elected officials; give them opportunities to teach a class or address students or staff. Record the presentations and make the audio or video available on school Web sites. Hold a regular luncheon or other event where government officials and teachers, administrators, student leaders, parent leaders, and others can meet one another and discuss important school-related issues. Offer student artwork and other materials to decorate local and regional government buildings and offices. Work with area government communicators and marketers to create information for use in government publications and placement on local and regional government Web sites. *Finally:* Always remember to invite local officials to school events and performances. And remember to thank them for their support of schools and students.

BOX 14.1

Example: Using Advisory Committees to Support School PR

Schools often turn to advisory committees (or task forces, commissions, advisory panels) to tap the expertise of leaders from all types of groups and organizations throughout the community.

No matter what they are called, properly structured and operated, advisory committees can be excellent ways to facilitate open communication between schools and their communities. But poorly structured and managed, such groups can quickly morph into generators of communication nightmares.

From the beginning, advisory committees need to have a clear and specific mandate, and members of the committees, as well as others interested in their work, need to understand and agree that their job is to advise. Advisory committees counsel and suggest ideas to help school leaders and staff make decisions.

One big problem: Schools too often fail to follow up on the work of advisory committees by explaining how the information and counsel the committee offered factored in final decisions. When a committee's advice isn't followed to the letter, volunteer advisors may feel dejected since their insight was "ignored." In fact, their work may have been extremely valuable to school decision makers, but the lack of ongoing communication failed to show how the work of the committee tied directly to final decisions. *Bottom line:* Communication about advisory group work needs to continue well after the committee has issued its final findings. Schools need to explain and help people understand how the insight and information collected during the fact-finding and decision-making process is being used.

Some ideas for getting the most from advisory groups:

- Write a concise and clear charge that sets specific parameters for the committee's work. Publish a clear timeline, with interim and final deadlines, for its work. Establish a timetable and interim deadlines for progress reports to the school board, administrative cabinet, or other governing body.
- Keep the size manageable. Large committees (often 15 or more people) may appear at the outset to be more inclusive, but the work of large groups can quickly become difficult to focus. Maintaining productivity and effectiveness suffers as the size of such groups expands.
- Make sure those serving are representative of the community interest important to the topic and issue being studied.
- Have staff adequately brief and prepare committee volunteers in the issue under review and their roles as committee members. Prepare background materials. Have a staff liaison support the group and provide access to other staff who may be helpful.
- Instruct the group in methods for running productive meetings—and avoiding meetings that disintegrate into "gripe sessions." Have a clear process for establishing

(Continued)

(Continued)

> group leadership, be it appointed or elected. Review and explain any rules or procedures to be followed in guiding the group's meetings and work.
> - Keep all proceedings as open to public review as possible. Always make final reports easily available. Put full copies on school Web sites, for example. *Also:* Report on them in school publications, discuss them at various school meetings, and release findings to area news media. Track and report on what is done with information in final reports as work on the issues continues.

Q&A: Dr. Don Bagin Talks About Key Communicators and School PR

Dr. Don Bagin founded the nationally recognized masters program in school public relations at Rowan University and directed the university's M.A. program in public relations for 40 years. A past president of the National School Public Relations Association, Dr. Bagin also founded and served as publisher of Communication Briefings, *a monthly communication-management newsletter that grew to serve more than 250,000 readers worldwide.*

Q: What are key communicator networks?

A: A key communicator network is really little more than a panel of influential communicators or opinion leaders who can have a real impact on the effectiveness of two-way school communication in any community. The group may be loose-knit or tightly structured. It may be small or large. It might operate districtwide, under the direction of the superintendent. Or it might operate more on a neighborhood level, under the direction of a principal or program administrator.

The bottom line is that a key communicator program helps schools get their messages out to the community quickly—and school staff can tap into the key communicator network for insights on what is being said by others in the community. This is one reason schools want to be flexible in how they structure key communicator programs. In some situations, large, formal programs—directed from a central office—may work best. In other instances, the efforts may be more decentralized with several key communicator networks built to serve individual schools and programs.

Q: Do visible community leaders make good key communicators?

A: Sometimes they do because of their positions in the community and their access to information and comments made by other leaders. But creating a good network of key communicators goes beyond just grabbing the names of those on a list of a community's formal power structure. Remember that key communicators are also people who are close to the ground in the day-to-day operation of a community at large. They are people who have a direct connection to a community's grapevine and are often the first people to be contacted by others when hot items begin to circulate on the rumor mill.

Given this characteristic, key communicators may include people not found on any typical organizational chart. They might include the operators of neighborhood businesses, such as hair salons, sandwich shops, or convenience stores. Leaders and key volunteers in faith organizations might be included as well.

The grassroots nature of their relationship to the community is what counts. Remember that nothing moves information more quickly than a grapevine. It may be tough for school leaders and other community leaders to tap directly into that line since people seeking to confirm or clarify rumors—and actually spreading rumors in the process—are more apt to repeat such information to those people in an informal power structure. This includes people they talk to on a regular basis and whose insight they trust—and this often does not include school officials.

By tapping into people at the grassroots level, schools can depend on key communicators to serve as a kind of early-warning system when rumors begin to brew—and they can put key communicators to work by offering the "real story" behind rumors that key communicators can spread on the community grapevine.

Q: How should someone begin to organize a key communicator network?

A: A good first step might be to think about how big a group you need to assemble. You want a group that is representative, but not one that is too large to manage. In general, groups of 12 to 15 members may be a good beginning. There's no real magic number, and nothing prevents you from increasing the size of a group once it is under way. Next you want to brainstorm who should be invited to serve. Who can you identify that both listens to and talks with key elements of the community?

The person running the network, whether a superintendent or principal or other program administrator, should then be the person to personally invite individuals to serve as key communicators. This invitation might best be done by letter. In this age of instant e-mail and phone communication, a letter might be seen as more personal in nature. A letter also offers the chance to carefully explain the school's plan and what a key communicator's obligations will be. Care should be taken to stress that this program, while organized, will not always require huge commitments of time devoted to meetings. By and large, the program will include a lot of informal communication between key communicators and their constituents, as well as school leaders. There will be a few meetings, but time commitments will go up and down based on communication needs and issues as they emerge.

Once key communicators have been identified, the program should begin with an organizational meeting. Here, key communicators can meet one another, and the specific roles they are being asked to fulfill can be explained. This is a simple process. Basically, key communicators should be encouraged to call or e-mail their school contact—that's the school official running this network—as soon as they hear something in the community that they think school officials should know or might need to address or clarify. They should also be encouraged to call any time they have personal questions or concerns.

Their contact information should be maintained in a phone or e-mail database, so that the school district can contact key communicators quickly, too, when news is about to break or important developments are about to be announced that are sure to spark discussions throughout the community. By arming key communicators with facts and data in advance, the school district can employ them to help squelch rumors and misinformation before they even begin.

It's also a good idea to communicate regularly with key communicators, perhaps with a note or e-mail once a month, if no pressing issues have made more frequent communication necessary. There will be quiet times when little is circulating on the community grapevine, and during these times, it's important to occasionally touch base with key communicators to make sure they're up-to-date on school news and mindful of the need to stay alert to what others are asking and saying about schools. Also, use these quiet times to ask their opinions on important school issues—even if the issues aren't creating controversy at the moment. Insights that key communicators offer may be helpful in other communication efforts.

There may be occasional follow-up meetings with key communicators, but these can be organized on an as-needed basis or held annually. Such events might be used to thank key communicators for their efforts and to report on accomplishments and contributions they have made.

15

Creating Your School PR Messages and Content

The rapid expansion of the media over the past generation has put many new tools at the fingertips of all school public relations efforts. *Think about all of the communication changes schools have dealt with in recent years.* First, desktop publishing sliced the cost and time needed to create professional-looking newsletters, brochures, and more. Then, Internet-driven online communications added e-mail, Web sites, e-newsletters, blogs, and more to the ever-growing options for disseminating news and information.

But one constant has survived all of this change: No matter what technique or media are used to communicate, the messages it carries will determine whether or not it succeeds. And messages, for the most part, depend on solid workaday writing that will attract readers, listeners, or viewers.

CREATING MESSAGES THAT WORK

Whether creating old-fashioned letters and flyers for parents or writing an e-newsletter to business leaders, the words and images you string together are key to, first, getting people to notice and read your message and, second, getting them to understand your message and do something as a result of it.

One major challenge: While many educators may have extensive training and experience in writing, it's often focused on administrative and programmatic writing that may not work well in public relations activities. For the type of passive, casual readers that make up most general audiences, education writing often is seen as overly complex and failing to offer any direct benefit to the reader.

The fix: Those who communicate on behalf of schools need to develop flexibility in style and tone when writing for public relations. In other words, they need to understand that different audiences have different communication styles and needs.

Before tapping any words into a keyboard, you should first assess your audiences. How are they comfortable communicating? What do they already know about the topic? Next, think about the copy about to be written. If successful, exactly what will it accomplish?

In a sense, the writer is establishing performance objectives for the copy and the messages it will carry—objectives that will both help to guide the content and style of the copy as it is created and set some expectations for results.

This process can begin by answering a simple set of questions:

- Should the copy seek only to inform the audience (simply offer information)?
- Should the copy seek to inform the audience *and* seek the audience's acceptance of the information (get agreement)?
- Should the copy seek to inform the audience *and* seek the audience's acceptance *and* seek action (get the audience to do something)?

Deciding what the copy will accomplish is essential to deciding the type of background information needed to be included in the message—and how much background information the audience will need. For strictly informational tasks, little or no background may be needed. For complex writing tasks—where the writer wants the reader to do something—much more background information may be needed in the quest to get agreement and action.

More planning questions:

- *Where will my copy be used?* Where the copy may eventually be used also will determine, to some extent, how much copy should be developed. But be careful at this step as there is a bit of a "chicken-and-egg" game going on when you consider messages and the types of media used (brochure, handbook, speech, Web page, and so on) to deliver them. *Example:* Let's say the plan is to write content for a brochure to introduce new school-day schedule for next year. As copy objectives are set, it may turn out that a brochure alone will work if you simply need to announce the new schedule. But if you want people to agree that the new schedule is a good idea, more content and more complex messages need to be developed—and a brochure alone may not be enough to do the trick. Face-to-face meetings, a series of newsletter articles, or some online content may have to be added to the plan to get awareness of and agreement on the new schedule.

- *Who's talking?* The outcome sought can also determine who should be the source of the information being provided. For simple, informative tasks, no source may be needed. It may suffice to simply communicate the information. But credibility of information sources grows more important for writers seeking to get agreement and action. A high school official—or the person asking for an action—may need to be quoted as an information source. Or other sources may be better suited to the copy depending on an audience's beliefs and biases. A parent leader, or a teacher, or a student will sometimes work better than a school official as a source of information in some copy, depending on the audience and the situation. Ask how hard your copy will have to work to cement your credibility. Who in the organization should be cited in my copy? Should I include data or quotes from outside sources?
- *What's my mood?* Finally, the copy's tone needs to accommodate the audience and support the outcome the copy seeks. Should terms and phrasing be formal or informal? Businesslike or neighborly? Instructive or elicitive?

LINKING MESSAGES TO NEEDS AND BELIEFS

There's an old rule of thumb employed by public relations practitioners: Communication efforts don't create messages that persuade people to do things. Rather, most public relations efforts focus on giving people reasons or methods for doing things they should be doing. In other words, messages supply evidence and options that help people persuade *themselves* to act, based on how they already think or believe. Successful messages help people link their behavior to their beliefs.

EXAMPLE: CREATING MESSAGES THAT SPARK ACTION

A school system might want to encourage parents to get more involved in their children's schoolwork. They use communications to stress that students do better when adults read to them at home—and when parents listen intently as children read to them.

But just communicating the command "read with your children" may do little more than stress parents—who already have many pressures on their time and may not easily see how they have the time or expertise to read with their children.

Properly constructed school messages can help parents resolve this conflict and get involved. This might be accomplished by simply communicating a list of common ways that children and parents can read together in everyday activities—and the benefits that will result when they do. *Examples:* creating a grocery list or chore list, reading the weekend movie schedule, writing up directions for a drive to Grandmother's house, and so on.

The bottom line: Simply telling parents that they should read to their children may do little more than make them feel uncomfortable or worse. This kind of communication doesn't go far enough. Offering a list of simple ways they can fulfill this task helps them see how they and their children can succeed—and how the school is a vital partner in the process.

Remember: When crafting messages, always say what you want audience members to do when they get the message—not just what you want them to know. Then evaluate how well the messages motivate and support the behavior you're trying to initiate.

PAY ATTENTION TO MESSAGE MEANINGS

The advertising adage "sell the sizzle, not the steak" is one worth ignoring. While school public relations efforts might have plenty of sizzle from time to time, the steak itself is what interests most people. Too much sizzle can actually detract from key messages. Messages need both steak and sizzle.

Some reasons: School public relations messages should establish realistic expectations—for both schools and the public. Undue hype and hyperbole will eventually work against school public relations efforts. The public in general and parents in particular are bright, are tuned in to many school issues, and have a keen sense of reality when picking through messages. Unrelenting media and online messages have created an oversensitivity to hard sell and hoopla.

Successful message development focuses on two issues:

1. What a message promises.

2. How that promise is packaged and delivered.

To work, messages need to be clear and delivered in a framework that speaks to the audiences' self-interest. They need to be compelling, but they also need to be credible.

Understanding this environment is critical to seeing the fine line that the public relations writer needs to navigate. Public relations messages—and the copy that carries them—need to be bold enough to attract the attention of busy readers but realistic enough to garner their confidence as well. Copy that's overly promotional may attract attention but quickly lose readership as credibility for the content never materializes. On the other hand, substantive copy with little hype can be very credible—but it doesn't matter since the boring presentation attracts no audience to begin with.

Messages need to give people a rationale and framework in which they can act comfortably. Messages need to take audience members to the point of action—in a way that doesn't overtly "push" them into action. The act—or desired behavior—needs to be the logical result achieved when a person reads or hears the message.

In short, successful messages must be realistic, honest, and convincing. They depend on the public relations writer's understanding the audience and having a clear grasp of what can and cannot be accomplished at any given time. Once the writer has a framework for what can be achieved—and has identified the possible objections that probably will be raised along the way—believable messages focused on the benefits and rewards of action can be crafted. And those messages are delivered in copy characterized by an appropriate tone and voice for the audience being addressed.

SOME SUGGESTIONS
FOR BUILDING SUCH MESSAGES

- Know your audience's beliefs and needs and accommodate them directly. Chances are good that many school audiences are already sold on the importance of schools and the value of supporting education. Messages then should seek to support and reinforce these already existing beliefs rather than trying to create new ones. In other words: Don't reinvent the wheel. Make the most of the knowledge and predispositions an audience already holds.
- Create a personal voice, not an institutional one. People generally want to communicate with other people—not buildings or systems or institutions. A recognizable, friendly voice is a potent catalyst for public relations that work. People respond warmly when they hear a trusted voice—even if the news is bad.
- Don't overreach in communication. While excitement may be contagious, getting overly excited or ambitious can work to create unreasonable expectations that may be difficult to meet. Make sure messages help audience members both see an eventual goal and have confidence that it can be reached.
- Doubts and objections sometimes result when audience members do not see the full value in a proposed suggestion or solution. When this happens, proposed solutions may create doubt and anxiety. The public relations writer needs to have a keen feel for where most of the audience stands on any given issue—and compose messages that work to highlight the value they offer and create a consensus on a solution.

BOX 15.1

How to Power Up School PR Messages

Stop and think about all of the messages being delivered by school systems every single day. People are logging on to school and district Web sites all the time and being bombarded with news, information, logos, slogans, images, and more. Local media carry news stories about decisions and events almost daily. School administrators and others are in the community attending meetings, delivering presentations, and answering questions. School newsletters, flyers, brochures, and more arrive in the mail, in the backpacks of students, or from the information racks in offices and lobbies. Other publications, memos, letters, and e-mails target employees in what, at times, may seem like a daily avalanche of news and information about schools and the school system.

Clearly, communication is a big business in any school system. Do public relations activities in your system make the most of the information that is flying about? Is there a plan to systematically reinforce key messages? Or is information sharing in your school system random—a kind of shotgun approach that simply shoots out information in the hope that some of it will be noticed, remembered, and acted upon?

Most schools enjoy a great deal of support and loyalty from those involved with them—especially parents. To some extent, this support for local schools may extend to the school system overall.

Schools and their districts can capitalize on the strength in these working relationships by crafting reinforcing messages that speak to the school's and school system's mission and the reputation it would like to hold among key audience members. To be effective, however, such overall or systemwide messages must be delivered and reinforced in a consistent manner by public relations activities throughout the school system—district-driven as well as individual school public relations efforts.

Most school systems need to compete for attention in a crowded communication marketplace. Parents and others are inundated with persuasive messages from all types of commercial and nonprofit organizations.

The bottom line: Single messages delivered randomly in school newsletters, popping up on school Web pages, or dropped into take-home flyers will all too easily get lost in the clamor of competing communications that school audiences must sift through daily.

Remember: Successful school public relations messages do more than get noticed—they get audiences to act on them.

For this to happen, public relations planning must isolate the school system's core missions or issues and find ways to link public relations messages to them. When this happens, public relations activities—over time—can more effectively hammer home key messages again and again.

Example: If the district's mission is to focus on student achievement for all learners, then public relations messages should find ways in which to tie into that theme. Logos or taglines related to the mission should be consistently displayed on all publications and other tactics systemwide.

Districtwide, key messages and supporting information should be developed for use by schools in their individual publications, Web sites, presentations, and other public relations activities. Conversely, public relations activities in local schools should provide fodder for messages in districtwide public relations efforts—offering examples and anecdotes that support how core missions are being achieved and the benefits they're generating for students and others.

In a sense, such reinforcement borrows a page from the marketing communicators' game plan by building a "brand" for schools with the proper images and reputations to support it. Incorporating such messages throughout a school system also can have a unifying effect—helping students, parents, employees, and others see how the commitment to excellence they feel in their school is part of a global initiative in the school system overall. When successful, such efforts diminish the "us versus them" feeling that can sometimes infiltrate local schools by helping people better see and understand the big picture and their roles in it. The good reputations local schools enjoy begin to support the system's reputation overall—while the strengths of the district work to reinforce the strengths of its schools.

WRITING FOR READERSHIP

Writing good public relations copy is about attracting and keeping readers. Unlike students in a classroom, parents at home or taxpayers in a community aren't required to read anything the school district creates. In fact, information disseminated by schools has to compete with all the other information bombarding audiences—slick direct-mail ads, riveting news stories, flashy TV ads, and more. Luckily, some parents might be a bit more motivated to read materials that come from schools—but others aren't. And seniors and others in the community with no direct connection to schools have virtually no incentive to pay attention to school messages.

To succeed, schools need to borrow from the tactics employed by public relations and marketing communication writers out to snag audience attention and keep it long enough to influence their behavior.

Three crucial first steps to creating copy that works:

1. Use small words.

2. Write short sentences.

3. Place sentences in short paragraphs.

Several readability formulas have been used by publishers and advertisers over the years to assess reading ease and comfort levels. One of the more popular ones, the Gunning-Fog Index, applies a formula to the average sentence length and percentage of large (three-syllable or more) words found in a selection of text to calculate a reading grade level. *The suggestion:* The lower the grade level, the greater the comfort level among people reading the text. The characteristics of this formula hold an important message for public relations writers. This readability test focuses on the importance of *using short sentences* and *using small words* to create copy that people will find *comfortable to read.*

It's important to note, however, that creating short sentences built with small words is not about writing simplistic messages. It is, rather, about conveying what often may be complex ideas and information with a great deal of precision, conciseness, and clarity—in the interest of successfully attracting readership.

Think of the old yarn about a tree falling in the forest. Does it make a noise if no one is there to hear it? Apply the same thinking to your messages. Do they make a difference if no one chooses to read or watch them? The answer to this question is a clear No! Messages are worthless without readership. Copy needs to have readership before it can succeed.

To increase the likelihood of generating readership, you should keep the following in mind as you create copy.

- Rely on short sentences, written in the active voice. There is no magic number for sentence length, and, in fact, using a variety of sentence lengths can be important to developing both a successful cadence and tone for the copy. However, public relations writers generally agree that average sentence lengths ranging between 15 and 20 words work well in typical copy. Remember, this is an average. Some sentences may, if justifiable, be longer than the average, and others may be shorter. But overall, sentences should average between 15 and 20 words. This means relying on simple sentences and avoiding complex, compound ones.
- Use short, familiar words. Suggestions vary on how to accomplish this. Some public relations writers might suggest using letter counts—urging that the majority of words be made up of seven or fewer characters. Others might suggest counting syllables, with the majority of words having less than three syllables. Whatever method, small, forceful words should always be used rather than lengthier ones with the same or similar meanings.

REVISING COPY TO STRENGTHEN MESSAGES

One secret to writing better public relations content to keep in mind: Understand that writing is a process, and learn to get the most from that process. Forget about writing perfect content in a first draft. Copy needs to be reviewed and edited—improved with each new revision.

Throughout this process, you—the writer—are analyzing content (the messages crafted in the copy) and structure (the ways in which the copy delivers its messages) to make sure the copy will be readable and, therefore, will attract readership.

Here are some suggestions to successfully revise copy:

Focus on Verbs

Verbs provide a sense of motion for readers and breathe life into copy. Strong active verbs can help convey a sense of urgency—a sense of importance to the topic being covered. But too often, first-draft copy tends to focus more on the subjects than on the objects of this action—the *doers* rather than what is being done.

Look for ways to replace those verbs that express no action. Often these include many so-called linking verbs, especially those in the *be* family, including *is, were, am, be, are, being, was, been.*

Example: "John is a parent volunteer at Lilac Middle School" *might become* "John serves as a parent volunteer at Lilac Middle School."

Example: "The district was awarded first place" *might become* "The district won first place."

Don't try to eliminate all of these verbs, but don't overload your copy with them either. Strong copy generally enjoys verb diversity.

Linking verbs and their close relatives sometimes creep into sentences when they simply aren't needed. By eliminating them during revisions, sentence lengths can be shortened—helping your goal of producing good readability

Example: "Joseph Smith, who is a teacher at Modern City High School, will retire next year" *might become* "Modern City High School teacher Joseph Smith will retire next year." (Do the math: 15 words in the original vs. 11 in the revision—roughly a 25 percent reduction on sentence length!)

Example: "Terry Jones, who is an honor student at Middletown Middle School, enjoys writing assignments that are difficult tasks" *might become* "Middletown Middle School honor student Terry Jones enjoys difficult writing assignments." (Do the math: 18 words in the original vs. 11 words in the revision!)

Finally, writers sometimes kill off the action in perfectly good verbs by adding extra words and turning these verbs into nouns or adjectives. Education writing frequently commits this infraction:

Example: "It is our expectation that more students will fail" *instead of* "We expect more students to fail."

Do the math on that example, too, and you will see that turning these verbs into nouns not only takes action out of the sentence, but it also makes the sentence longer. (In the example above, the first sentence has nearly twice as many words as the second, 10 words vs. 6.)

Tip: A couple of signs offer clues to verb problems in copy. Look for these as you revise: Words ending in *ance, ence, ing, ion,* and *ment* can signal nouns that might be verbs. *Examples:* "We arrived at an agreement" *might be better as* "We agreed." *Another:* "The principal gave an explanation of the new attendance policy" *might be better as* "The principal explained the new attendance policy." Also look for words following the verb *made.* These might include *made a reservation* (reserved), "made a decision" (*decided*), or "made a change" (*changed*).

Focus on Prepositions

Taking some prepositions out of copy can reduce overall sentence length. Here again, you probably don't want to eliminate all prepositions in the interest of offering variety and developing the right cadence for your copy.

Example: "The principal *of* the school told the faculty *of* the science department to expect an increase *of* 10 percent *in* student enrollment" *might become* "The school's principal told the science-department faculty to expect a 10 percent student enrollment increase." (Here again, sentence length improves dramatically—22 words vs. 16 words.)

Example: "We have continued a redistricting of attendance boundaries based on policies of the board" *might become* "We have continued attendance-boundary redistricting based on board policies."

Look for these common prepositions: *aboard, about, above, across, after, against, along, among, around, at, before, behind, below, beneath, beside, besides, between, beyond, concerning, despite, during, except, excluding, following, for, from, in, inside, into, like, near, of, on, onto, over, regarding, since, than, through, toward, towards, under, underneath, until, up, upon, with, within, without.*

Focus on Structures

Strong sentence structures allow readers to quickly decipher their meaning as verbs convey a strong sense of the action. Weaker structures, encumbered by needless phrases including pronouns and linking verbs, increase sentence length and complexity. Such structures are common in first-draft writing, but can easily be eliminated when copy is edited and revised. *One tip:* Often sentences beginning with "there is" or "there are" signal opportunities for revision.

Example: "There is no evidence in the assessment to support addition remedial instruction" *might become* "Nothing in the assessment supports additional remedial instruction."

Example: "There are several new employees who will be joining us as we begin the new school year" *might become* "Several new employees will join us in the new school year."

Focus on Positives

Teachers know that instructing students on *what to do* generally works better than showing them *what not to do*. The same holds true in developing copy for public relations content. People tend to react better to positive messages—it's easier to figure out what a person should do when the message is crafted in a positive way.

But negatives in a public relations message go beyond telling people what not to do. Unintended negative tones can be created in messages when explaining basic policies and procedures.

Example: "We cannot give you the grades until you sign the release form" *might work better as* "We'll give you the grades as soon as you sign the release form."

Example: "The main office closes at 4 p.m." *might be better as* "The main office is open until 4 p.m."

Example: "Transportation won't be provided to those students living within one mile of the school" *might be better as* "All students living a mile or more from the school receive transportation."

Focus on Voice

Education writing often uses the passive voice (basically: a verb's past participle and any form of the verb *to be*). Such writing shifts the focus of the action in the sentence from the doer of the action to the recipient of it. *Consider this example:*

Active: "The dog bit the boy."

Passive: "The boy was bitten by the dog."

There may be times when you want to use the passive voice to add emphasis for the recipient of the action. *For example:* "Fifty students were helped by the new program." In this sentence, you might want to emphasize the students over the program.

But in most cases, using the active voice results in shorter sentences that most people will find easier to read.

Example: "The faculty award was given to Brenda Most at graduation" *might become* "Brenda Most received the faculty award at graduation."

Example: "According to parent input, a school should be built in which state-of-the-art technology would be made available for students and staff" *might become* "Parent input suggests the new school should offer students and staff state-of-the-art technology."

Consider: Active voice writing employs the basic sentence structure of subject, verb, and object ("I see you"). Passive voice rearranges this order and forces the reader to do more work to figure out who is doing what to whom ("You are the person I see").

Passive voice can make copy longer and, therefore, make it "seem harder" to read. And remember, reading public relations content is an *option* for most people. To succeed, the public relations writer needs to construct copy that is easy to read and has a high level of benefit for the audience.

TRANSITIONS: SHIFTING GEARS BETWEEN IDEAS

Simply listing key ideas and information supporting messages will not be enough to drive readers to the level of understanding and action you are seeking. Often, strategic transitions are needed to help connect ideas and build the foundation of logic that readers need.

Many writers see transitions as simply devices to connect compound sentences or ideas. The public relations writer, however, knows that transitions can be used more like the transmission in the car—that is, they can smoothly shift from gear to gear as the "message" accelerates and decelerates along an information highway.

Like a well-functioning transmission, the work of transitions in good copy is barely noticed by the reader. Consider this passage:

The work done by dedicated River City teachers supports student excellence. They face many obstacles, including getting resources for students. They deal with many students posing significant challenges. They deal with many tough situations. They have few opportunities to share their work. Parents and others may not understand the good work they accomplish in this environment.

Now consider how the same passage works with a few well-placed transitions:

The work done by dedicated River City teachers supports student excellence. *But* they face many obstacles, include getting resources for students. *And* they deal with many students posing significant challenges. *In short,* they deal with many tough situations. *However,* they have few opportunities to share their work. *As a result,* parents and others may not understand the good work they accomplish in this environment.

In the original, several main points are simply strung together like beads on a string. But in the revision, note how the transitions work to unify the key ideas in the message and logically build toward the conclusion the writer wants the reader to make.

Public relations writers rely on transitions in copy when building messages to help introduce new ideas or directions (*so, as a result, then, accordingly, clearly,* and so on).

They also use transitions to move or shift through various points (*also, and, but, for instance, furthermore,* and so on). And transitions can be used to help readers conclude key points (*thus, therefore, in short, the bottom line, in conclusion,* and so on).

Some typical transition groups to use:

Relationships: *above, across, adjacent to, around, behind, below, beside, beyond, closer to, far from, nearby, opposite to, over*

Timing: *as soon as, before, during, earlier, immediately, later, meanwhile, soon, until, when*

Order: *after, again, finally, first, next, second, soon, subsequently, then, third*

Comparisons: *although, but, even though, for example, however, in contrast, in fact, in the same way, in the same manner, like, likewise, similarly, nevertheless, on the other hand, otherwise, whereas, yet*

Emphasis: *again, also, another, as a result, because, consequently, finally, for this reason, furthermore, in addition, in brief, in short, in summary, moreover, since, therefore, thus*

ASSURING MESSAGE TRANSPARENCY

Public relations messages need honesty and transparency to work—not at all what's suggested by the image of spin and obfuscation public relations often has. The key to audience acceptance is message credibility. The audience must develop a high level of trust in both the source and content of the message.

Message transparency—or clarity—is vital to the process. Fuzzy writing is a problem that afflicts many organization communicators. For reasons of politeness or politics, writers in organizations sometime shy away from being too specific. *The result:* A principal might use a phrase such as "student incident" when discussing an issue. A more specific description might be "student altercation." And a clear description might be "fight in the cafeteria."

Abstract words and phrases may sometimes be necessary when discussing overall views or broad concepts. But generally, nonspecific terms can work against writers by creating the perception of glossing over serious or negative issues.

Some examples:

Instead of "The program offers many amazing things," *try* "The program offers specific exercises to boost spelling skills."

Instead of "We selected this video because of its reputation," *try* "We selected this video because more than 100 other schools recommended it."

Instead of "It appears all or nearly all students may be able to participate in the program," *try* "We're hopeful as many students as possible will be able to participate in the program."

Remember: Nonspecific wording can damage message and source credibility—it can create the appearance of insincerity or deception.

Wordiness is one final area affecting message transparency. Here, straightforward inattention—not working to eliminate redundancies or unnecessary wordiness in first-draft copy—can damage clarity and hurt the performance of messages.

Example: "It is absolutely essential to determine if we should make a final decision on the budget" *might work better as* "We must decide on the budget."

Example: "Teachers know from past classroom experience that students sometimes revert back to old behaviors" *might work better as* "Teachers know from classroom experience that students sometime revert to past behaviors."

Some common redundant phrases to avoid:

absolutely necessary	advance reservations
actual experience	basic fundamentals
actual facts	basic necessities
advance forward	close proximity
advance planning	completely destroyed
advance preview	completely eliminate

completely engulfed

controversial issue

each and every

earlier in time

eliminate altogether

final conclusion

final outcome

had done previously

introduced a new

originally created

past history

past memories

repeat again

reply back

retreat back

revert back

still persists

still remains

true facts

ultimate goal

unexpected emergency

unexpected surprise

unintentional mistake

very unique

16

Delivering Your School PR Messages and Content

In Print and Online

ORGANIZING PR TACTICS

The list of public relations tactics used to deliver messages and content is long—and growing. Emerging communication technology continues to open new options for both collecting feedback and disseminating information. These advances include newer techniques (such as online RSS feeds for instantly delivering news and podcasts to subscribers) as well as more traditional techniques now available to schools because technology advances have cut their cost or reduced the level of technical skill needed to use them (online surveys and e-newsletters, for example).

BOX 16.1

Checklist: Typical Print and Online School PR Tactics

Consider this checklist that includes many of the print and online message-delivery options for school public relations efforts:

(Continued)

(Continued)

Newsletters

Brochures and pamphlets

Flyers

Letters (mass and personal)

Posters

Handbooks

Calendars

Policy and procedure manuals

Fact sheets and Q&A sheets

Bulletin and message boards

Surveys and polls

Blast or broadcast communications (telephone, text messaging, and e-mail)

Hotlines and answer lines

District, school, and special purpose Web sites

E-mail

E-newsletters

Listservs and discussion groups

Online surveys and feedback forms

Database-driven information retrieval (budgets, attendance boundaries, and so on)

Online recruitment and registration materials (students and parents)

Online recruitment materials (staff positions)

Streaming video and audio

Downloadable podcasts (video and audio)

RSS and other news subscription services

Blogs and diaries

Online grade books and lesson plans

News releases

Media backgrounders

Media tours

News conferences

Talk show appearances

Cable TV programming

Public service announcements

Ads (print, broadcast, and online)

Special events

Open houses, tours, and orientations

Fairs and festivals

Fundraising events

Commencements and awards ceremonies

Groundbreakings and ribbon cuttings

Anniversaries, retirements, and other milestone celebrations

New-year and end-of-year gatherings

Community group speeches and presentations

Workshops and seminars

Student performances and presentations

Schools often use more of these public relations tactics than they sometimes realize—since some of these efforts may, over time, be seen more as obligatory administrative functions rather than public relations opportunities.

Compiling a sample of communication activities now under way can help public relations planners begin to organize their efforts and build synergy among them.

- **Step 1:** Using the list above as a guide, collect copies or samples representing all of your public relations activities over the past year.
- **Step 2:** Look through the pile of material and consider how well the materials work together to create a consistent look and feel for the school or school system (brand building). What in these materials repeats and reinforces key school and district messages? Be brutal. In total, do these materials represent the work of a comprehensive public relations effort—or do they look more like a random collection of isolated, unrelated single-purpose efforts?
- **Step 3:** Consider the short- and long-term impacts of these efforts. Who is using these materials—and how do I know they are using them? How are the materials being used? If we stopped a tactic, how long would it take before someone noticed? Do we need more tactics—or would we be better served to reduce the tactics now being used? *One tip:* Try writing a succinct, one- or two-sentence "purpose statement" for each item. If a meaningful statement can't be written, the item might not be needed.

While this exercise falls far short of being a full and formal assessment of ongoing public relations activity, it can be an important start to getting a handle on the effort now being invested in public relations. It can also help to uncover insights on how some changes in messaging and branding can improve the efficiency and effectiveness of efforts already under way. And it can reveal errors where public relations efforts may be lacking or need expanding.

COMMUNICATING THROUGH DESIGN

Printed and online materials need to be designed. Paper stock (or page backgrounds), font colors, column widths, page (or screen) sizes, folds, type fonts, type sizes, paragraph indents and spacing, photos and art, lines and rules, and more all play roles in how well a tactic delivers its message.

As a result, the public relations planner needs to be aware of much more than the creativity used to forge design—good design effectively delivers messages. Good design both attracts readers and viewers and is easy to navigate or read.

Bad functional design can destroy a tactic's ability to deliver an otherwise valuable message. Good functional design can strengthen the success of message delivery.

This issue grows even more complex when audience needs and behaviors are considered. Different audiences may relate differently not only to communication tactics themselves but to the various design options available for those tactics. Some audiences may find larger type sizes easier to read. Other audiences may find fresh designs creative and inspiring, while other audiences may view them as nontraditional and less credible.

How people relate to and use various communication tactics can be an important aspect also in evaluating how they should be designed and used.

For example: Younger people might have more interest in receiving information through online communication than they might from senior citizens. This is not to say that seniors should be ignored in online communications, but online efforts aimed at seniors may need different designs to function better for them. A school might find, for instance, that e-mail is an effective method for communicating quickly with students and young parents—since most use e-mail and check it frequently throughout the day. Older individuals might use e-mail but check it less often—meaning you can reach them with e-mail, but it may not be the best device for communicating quickly. Thus, when a tactic needs to be designed to accommodate speed and urgency, e-mail blasts might work for some audiences but not others.

These individual preferences pose several challenges and opportunities for school public relations planners; while new communication options have expanded the arsenal of tactics available for public relations efforts, these new practices have not, for the most part, supplanted any traditional methods used in public relations programming. Online and e-publications now let school public relations efforts communicate more quickly, more frequently, and at less cost than older print options, but they cannot necessarily supplant all print publications.

The good news: Schools have more options than ever for sending information to and receiving information from important audiences quickly.

The bad news: The increasing complexities of media choices combined with the rapid-fire pace of ongoing communication mean public relations planning and assessment are increasingly essential to avert disaster and ensure success.

The bottom line: Conventional wisdom and gut feeling no longer are enough to guide public relations strategy.

ACCOMMODATE HOW PEOPLE READ

Think about how you go through your own mail every day—or how you behave when opening your e-mail every morning. If you're like most people, chances are you do not start with the first item and read it thoroughly before moving on to the next. Reading, for most people, involves making a lot of decisions—decisions made as they skim quickly through content, slowing to scan some things in a bit more detail, stopping to read a few things carefully, and totally ignoring others.

The challenge for school public relations tools:

- How do design and content work together to accommodate the skimming most people do when reading? What in the design and content draws the reader's attention to key points and encourages them to stop and read in greater detail?
- What in headlines, subheads, opening paragraphs, and highlighted "boxes" and "blurbs" communicates key messages quickly to these fast-moving scanners?
- What among these attention-getting graphic and design items seems beneficial enough to get people to stop and read in more detail?

This is often what is meant when public relations practitioners talk about "packaging" copy or content. It's not enough to write a great newsletter story or terrific brochure copy. The copy then needs to be packaged within a publication or Web page in a way that will both attract and hold readers. Good design supports readership. Bad design does not.

IDEAS FOR FACILITATING COMMUNICATION

School public relations efforts rely on both visual and print techniques to deliver messages. Such deliveries may be static or moving. They may be one-way or two-way. But no matter what ultimate direction they take, certain design considerations can help to improve the ease with which audience members read or view the important messages being delivered.

These considerations can work to improve the legibility of the piece, the clarity of the presentation. These considerations can work to improve the so-called reader-friendliness of a piece—that is, the degree to which users find the piece appealing and easy to navigate through.

Some suggestions:

- At the outset, approach a design as a method for helping readers see and appreciate the message being sent. Design should clearly appeal to the reader's self-interest (perhaps with a clear, bold headline) and communicate that it is coming from your school or school system (perhaps with appealing, consistently used and recognizable logos or images).

- Functional designs avoid elements that might interfere with readership. *Examples:* They avoid intricate background images or stark background colors on Web pages or printed pieces. These interfere with the ease of reading content. They also avoid intricate fonts that may be more difficult to decipher than more common fonts. Avoid type that is too big or too small to read comfortably. *Best bet:* Always research your audiences, if only informally. Convene a few focus panels to react to designs using a mix of font types. Without explaining the differences, see what reactions they have to your designs. And don't be surprised if different demographic groups (different ages, education levels, and so on) react differently.

- Don't wear out the options your design software offers. One problem with the explosion of desktop and Web-content design programs is the wide array of design options put at the fingertips of everyone using the software. Just because an option exists does not mean it needs to be used. *Some basic advice:* Stick to a limited number of fonts in any design—perhaps one font family for body text and another for headlines and subheads. Vary headline sizes to place greater emphasis on one headline over another (helping to guide the reader), but have a system to do this so there is some uniformity to headline sizes throughout a publication or series of Web pages.

- Use special features, such as italic or boldface type, to judiciously emphasize certain words or phrases. Don't overuse it by placing large passages in all italic or all boldface fonts. *The simple reason:*

Large passages in italic or boldface fonts simply are more difficult to read—meaning people are actually more likely to skim through those passages or skip them completely rather than focus on them.

- Avoid setting large areas of copy in reverse text as well (this is where white text, for example, is run on a black background). Large blocks of reversed text often are difficult to read. Instead, save the use of blocks of reversed text for short headlines or comments that you want to stand out. If you can use color, consider running the text in a contrasting, easy-to-read color instead of white. Many designers use yellow text, for example, on a black background to attract attention. But like any such attention-grabbing tool, it should be used sparsely and to achieve a specific effect. Overusing any such technique will dilute its effectiveness.

- All caps and small caps should be avoided in long text passages, too. Use of all caps and small caps in long passages creates the visual effect of a text block. Upper- and lowercase type creates visual relief and cues for readers—a natural landscape of valleys and ridges that is more comfortable to read.

- Columns and alignments can influence readability too. For print publications, many readability experts suggest using copy that is justified on the left side of the column but not on the right. (This is sometimes referred to as "ragged right" alignment.) Letter-sized pages generally are broken into two or three columns to improve readability. But type size should relate to column width. In general, the wider the column, the larger the font size should be. In general terms, 11-point or 12-point text works best in a three-column design on a standard-sized page. A two-column design might work better with 12-point or 14-point text. Many Web pages lack multiple columns—suggesting that smaller font sizes should especially be avoided in many online designs.

- In print, the design can control exactly how the page will look when printed and presented to the reader. But there is little control when it comes to designing pages that will be used online. The viewer's computer and its Internet browser preferences, as well as the size of the user's computer monitor, will influence what some page components will look like when they load. This means that print and online designs, while they may be similar, should be developed and evaluated separately. If controlling the precise look of a publication or document online is essential, or the ability for users to easily print it is important, it might be offered online in the commonly used PDF file format.

- Value open space. So-called white space (or unused space) is, in fact, an important design element. Open space can bring attention to the items and content it surrounds. Open space also can "air out" a presentation, making it appear to be less dense and thus less intimidating to a potential reader. Sometimes schools, perhaps in the interest of spending tax dollars wisely, seem to think that every inch of content area needs to be crammed with information or images. In fact, the better use of tax dollars might be leaving some space unused—in the interest of creating public relations materials that work. Beyond intimidating readers, crowded designs fail to give users and readers a logical starting place on the page. People looking at a crowded page are given no sense of direction or navigation and thus aren't sure where to begin. They may then, in fact, simply pass by the information, choosing not to begin at all.

- Make sure text and design work together. *One way:* Use a variety of article lengths to present information. Instead of a single long article on a topic, consider a shorter main article with key points. Support the article with a "sidebar" that perhaps presents a list of key data or a timeline, and a very brief "boxed" article, including one or two tips or suggestions related to the story. Breaking up long stories gives readers more options as they scan text—making content less imposing. *In addition:* A collection of different-sized articles on a single topic, when nested together, gives you more design options to create an appealing page than a single long article does. *Remember:* Long articles look deadly and many readers will avoid them. *Some rules of thumb for many school publications:* Keep articles at 500 words or fewer. Try not to jump stories to second pages. Use headlines and subheads to provide information and help readers navigate through content.
- Graphic devices can also be used to help break up text sections and offer navigational clues to readers. Bulleted lists are an excellent way to help readers skim quickly through key points. Using lines or "rules" to set off or box in key points and quotes can work well, too.
- Use photos, art, and illustrations to support text and aid readers as they move through your content. *Keep in mind:* Photos and other illustrations are devices to aid readers—they are not simply design elements used to enhance the look of a page. They should be used only for a specific strategic communication purpose. Captions (or "cutlines") under photographs should be written with some key information to attract skimmers to the story the photo supports. Captions should not simply identify who or what is in the photo. That assumes the person looking at the page has already read the accompanying article. Graphs and charts also should be run with captions—lacking such information, the reader has to "figure out" how to decipher the chart.
- *A word about permissions:* Most school systems have clear policies in place that meet local and federal laws governing privacy—as well as accommodating the security issues that may arise when using student or staff images in public relations materials. Many schools

employ "opt out" programs when parents register their children for school—that is, parents give their permission for their children's images to be used in such activities unless they "opt out" when registering. Other systems require that permission slips be signed whenever student or staff photos will be used in print or online communications. Whatever procedure your school district uses, make sure your use of local images adhere to these policies. All staff who use such images need to follow these policies too (this includes teachers, administrative assistants, and others who may be developing their own public relations tools). Organizations such as the National School Public Relations Association (www.nspra.org) and its local chapters can help to supply information on how districts in your region handle these kinds of issues. Generally, the school district attorney can address questions as well.

- Digital photography has made capturing photos to accompany public relations publications and Web sites much easier and less expensive than just a few years ago. But it has also increased the chance that amateur errors can creep into the process. To get good photos, focus on capturing true candid shots that reveal people engaged in their work or study. Take a lot of photographs and use the best one. Avoid large group shots. Instead, limit photographs to one or two people to show personality—or hundreds of people to show effect. Middle-sized group shots are neither personal nor effective. Avoid staged-looking photographs—that is, handshaking shots, sitting-behind-the-desk or standing-behind the-lectern shots, people pointing to something, and so on. *Also:* Use available photo editing programs (such as Adobe Photoshop or Microsoft Picture Manager) to make even simple changes that significantly improve photos. Cropping photos, for example, can remove distracting background images and give a greater focus to the person or action in the photo.

- Charts and graphs should be simple and communicate quickly. They should be used to support one key point—whether being used alone or in conjunction with an accompanying story. Bar graphs are generally considered to be more easily read than more involved charts (such as pie charts). Data in charts should be presented in ascending or descending order whenever possible. In other words, don't mix data forcing readers to decipher and relate it. Arrange data to convey and reinforce a clear point or trend.

- Think of page designs as a combination of modules—that is, each element on a page (blocks and boxes of text, headlines, subheads, logos, photos, charts, lines, and so on) is its own device and subject to its own design review. Overall page design, then, becomes the effective arrangement of each of these units on a grid—the page.

HEADLINES NEED SPECIAL ATTENTION

Too often headlines get treated as an afterthought—tossed on an article at the last minute with words perhaps chosen more for their ability to fit on the page than their ability to attract readers and sell the story.

Headlines make a promise: They telegraph to the reader what the story is about. They make an implied promise that the story must then deliver on.

But headlines have a kind of marketing function as well. That is, a headline must also subtly sell the story while attracting the reader. And all of this must be accomplished in just a few words. For example, consider this headline:

Impressive Number of Scholarships Given to Seniors This Year

Nice. But not too specific and not all that exciting. It's kind of what a reader would *expect* to hear from schools—but remember that good news often gives us the *unexpected*. Now consider this revision:

Record Set: Seniors Earn More Than $1 Million in Scholarships

The more specific and energetic revision does a better job of announcing what the story is about and creating the kind of excitement needed to attract readers to it.

Think about possible headlines as you write copy. Place a draft headline on a story when you begin—but go back and spend time writing a final headline once the text is completed.

As you revise headlines, think how best to make a bold statement in a few words. Consider synonyms of key words in the draft headlines to shorten or enliven them.

Basic rules on grammar, punctuation, and capitalization can vary in headlines, too. *Some guidelines:*

- Publications generally employ one of two styles for capitalization in headlines. *Up-style* more or less places an initial capital letter on all words—except articles (*the, a,* and so on) and prepositions of three or fewer letters (*for* and *on* would be lowercase, for example, while *Over* and *Under* would be uppercase). Up-style is considered more formal by many designers. *Down-style* headlines capitalize the first word in the headline as well as any proper nouns. Down-style is considered less formal by many.

  Up-style example: School Budget Committee Formed for Next Year

  Down-style example: School budget committee formed for next year

  School publications and Web pages can use either style. But whichever they choose should be used consistently throughout all materials.

- Some punctuation rules differ for headlines. Periods are not used except in abbreviations (which generally should be avoided anyway in headlines). Conjunctions sometimes are replaced by commas (*Teachers, students win awards*). In two-line headlines, semicolons can be used to separate two distinct but related thoughts (*School budget set; new teachers hired*). Quotation marks are single, not double as they are in text (*Superintendent commends 'academic excellence'*). Dollar signs are used for money figures and large numbers can be abbreviated (*Budget faces $1 million shortfall*).
- The tense used in headlines often confounds new public relations writers who have no journalistic background. *Here's why:* Even though stories often talk about events that have already occurred, headlines generally are written in the present or future tense. The use of present tense in headlines talking about past events might be viewed as helping to communicate a sense of immediacy or urgency. *For example:* A story about the board's budget approval last night would read *Board approves budget*—not *Board approved budget*.

DON'T BE ANONYMOUS

While mastheads or nameplates are generally associated with large commercial publications, such as newspapers and magazines, a brief masthead (or call it a staff box) should be included in many regular school publications (such as newsletters and e-newsletters). All school publications should be officially identified as school publications. A standard masthead offering the following items can be designed to do this:

The name of the publication and its publisher (the school district as well as the name of the local school for a school newsletter).

The name of the "editor" or person in charge of the publication, as well as other key persons helping to create it.

Contact information for offering comments and feedback, including postal and e-mail addresses, Web addresses, and phone numbers.

A purpose or mission statement for the publication. A one- or two-sentence summary of how the publication serves readers.

CONSISTENCY CREATES CREDIBILITY

Consistency in design helps to brand schools and creates a familiarity that builds credibility for public relations materials over time. Consistency in scheduling is crucial to building credibility as well. In other words, publication schedules create an implied promise to readers that needs to be upheld. This means monthly publications should appear on time every month. In fact, all regular publications should adhere to their schedules and be updated in a timely fashion.

Failing to produce publications on time communicates lack of importance for their contents and perhaps even an indifference to their readership. This slight is rarely intentional, but it's real nonetheless.

Even worse, in times of crisis when public relations materials are desperately needed to deliver urgent information, the loss of credibility created by an on-again, off-again publishing schedule can hurt effectiveness. Publications and other public relations materials that appear on an as-needed basis signal the school's or school district's interest in meeting its own communication agenda and not an interest in regularly addressing the readers' needs. In other words, people may begin to think the school is communicating only when it wants or needs something, not as an ongoing process to inform and engage its audiences.

This doesn't mean that special-issue or one-time publications can't be created in certain situations. But such efforts should tie in to ongoing publication efforts. A special bulletin or alert might be created when crucial news breaks between monthly newsletters, for example, but the bulletin will enjoy greater credibility if it is announced as a special issue of the newsletter. It can also promise more information or follow up information in the newsletter's next regular issue.

The bottom line: Public relations materials, both in print and online, need a commitment to follow a regular, timely, and ongoing effort. Such a schedule is essential to showing the seriousness of the system's dedication to two-way communication and the true audience engagement it fosters.

PACKAGE YOUR INFORMATION

It's no surprise that many educators are not graphic or online designers, but they do spend a great deal of time communicating. And how they present their ideas in publications, presentations, and reports—in person, in print, and online—has a great deal to do with their ultimate success as educators and as advocates for the schools and programs.

The bottom line: How information is packaged is an important part of the communication process, and anyone whose job involves communication should have at least an appreciation of how design and content should work together to accommodate communication.

This doesn't mean you need to go back to school to get a degree in design. It does suggest, however, that some professional development on design issues might be a good idea. Educators communicating on behalf of schools should be fluent in basic design concepts to direct the design of their own public relations materials and effectively work with professional communicators and designers who are helping you develop or improve materials.

Many area colleges offer professional development workshops (some are even offered online) that cover basic design concepts. Many self-help books exist on the topic, as well.

If you have a designer on staff—or work with a freelance designer—consider asking that person to develop some brief staff training on key design issues for you and others. Remember that many school staff members prepare communication materials—letters and announcements to be sent home, bulletin boards, message boards, e-mails to outsiders, and so on—that should be "designed" to communicate well.

Beyond getting some training, you might also simply begin to observe what others are doing when it comes to the design of their public relations tools. When reviewing successful materials of others, pay attention to how the material is designed, and look for tactics that might be used to help improve your materials.

Also: Collect and study the award-winning work of other schools. The National School Public Relations Association (NSPRA) sponsors an annual awards program to recognize excellence in school public relations tools of all sorts. The names and contact information for winning school systems are posted on the organization's Web site each year. (Learn more at www.nspra.org.) In addition, many NSPRA regional and state chapters run similar awards programs each year. A list of local chapters is available on NSPRA's Web site, as well.

Templates and design guidelines can be invaluable to all school staff involved in public relations efforts. Since technology has put the ability to create public relations materials into the hands of anyone who can operate a computer, people with little or no writing or design background may find themselves churning out public relations materials. But this is a good thing! All school staff members have crucial communication roles, and they need to be supported in them if they are to be held accountable for them. Along with offering basic training, supplying ready-made templates for newsletters, brochures, PowerPoint presentations, and Web pages can help staff members create more effective materials and begin to build a consistent look to materials throughout the school system. A list of style guidelines would also help people make basic choices when designing, such as where to place logos, what colors and fonts are preferred, and contact or identifying information that should be included on all official publications.

BOX 16.2

School PR Quick Tips: Print and Online

- Look for ways to capture video at important events and meetings. Video can be offered to the media to use in their coverage or on news Web sites. It can be streamed or offered as podcasts on your own Web site. It might offer background or support footage to future communication projects. It might be edited down to provide brief informational podcasts or other instructional snippets on certain issues.

(Continued)

(Continued)

- Create a file (paper or on your computer) titled "story ideas." Then keep an eye out for possible stories to use in your public relations efforts when talking to people, reading e-mail and memos, scanning the news media, and attending staff meetings. Jot quick reminders in your "story ideas" file, and review them when you need content for newsletters, Web pages, or presentations.

- Avoid "jumping" or continuing a story in a newsletter or brochure from one page to another. *Reason:* Readership always falls off, and many people never jump to finish the story. Edit relentlessly in an effort to keep the story to one page. If you must jump the story, make sure crucial information is in the first section of the story.

- Boost readability of newsletters and other publications by helping readers quickly prioritize and categorize information. *How:* Group related information on the same page or facing pages. Use regular headings (*examples:* Breaking News, Coming Soon, Important Dates, and so on). Keep articles short. Use bulleted lists and graphics to accommodate scanners. *Tip:* Offer quick summaries of complex issues, and point readers to more in-depth information on your Web site.

- Look for ways to maximize effort on major publications with spin-offs. *Example:* Can parts of an annual report be spun off to serve as school publications on various topics covered in the report? Can segments be quickly redesigned to serve as Web pages? Can some illustrations be enlarged for bulletin boards or poster displays?

- To find more typos when proofing Web and publication copy, try reading the copy backwards one word at a time. Also, try reading it out loud. Both techniques can slow you down while proofing and help you spot errors you might otherwise read past. *Additional tip:* Always dial phone numbers and visit Web addresses listed one final time—to make sure they are accurate.

- Consider running a photo contest among employees or students to generate shots of facilities or candid shots of staff and students for Web or publication use. It could boost morale, recognize homegrown talent, and generate some good photography for your products. *Just remember:* Always get releases from those photographed before using any photos.

- Don't make the "penny-wise-pound-foolish" mistake of printing too few copies of anything. In general, additional printed copies are very inexpensive when produced as part of an initial print run.

- Try running an ongoing contest with a small prize for the first person reporting a bad link or outdated material appearing on your Web site. It's an easy way to get rid of outdated content—and it shows you care about keeping content current.

- Use subheads as more than graphic devices to break up long segments of copy. For those simply scanning an article, publication or Web page subheads can tell a story of their own if coordinated to do so. *Consider:* Subheads are an important copy device, alerting readers to key points and, ideally, encouraging them to stop scanning and start reading.

- When mailing or e-mailing a batch of material, be sure to include yourself at a home address or personal e-mail address—so you can judge if and how quickly the material was delivered.
- Make sure you can answer the question "How do I know people are reading this?" for every publication you produce. Include feedback or comment cards and coupons, e-mail links, and telephone numbers to encourage response. *Also:* Conduct occasional informal readership polls or convene a focus group panel of readers to get their reactions.
- Want to get more people to volunteer to write your publications? Consider offering bylines or credit lines to staff or students who supply material. Offer certificates or other expressions of appreciation to those who contribute.
- If volunteers creating content have trouble meeting your deadlines, consider these strategies. Make sure deadlines are realistic—get their involvement in setting deadlines. Try incremental deadlines—drafts due on one date, final copy on another. Have a backup plan, to avoid disaster if deadlines are missed.
- Put key contact information (phone numbers, addresses, or feedback links) at the bottom of all publications and Web pages—so people can offer feedback quickly.
- Use charts and graphs whenever possible to help people visualize data. *Remember:* People can generally decipher bar graphs faster than pie charts. Colors, especially distinct contrasting colors, will communicate in graphs and charts more easily than shades of gray.
- When designing a newsletter or brochure, make sure you pay as much attention to the back page or panel as you do the front page or panel. *Reason:* Readers often turn the publication over to the back page before opening or unfolding it. *Result:* A back page or panel may get nearly as much initial reader attention as a front page or panel.
- Make sure school and district Web sites are ready to handle breaking news when a crisis strikes. *One reason:* More and more people—and the news media—are turning to Web sites for breaking information on developing issues. *Some possible online items:* updates about a breaking crisis and steps taken to safeguard students; latest news releases, fact sheets, official statements, and media advisories; advice and suggestions for helping children and others cope with crises—including links to other sources with advice and resources.

17

Delivering Your School PR Messages and Content

In the News Media

Whether you are working directly with the news media or working with a school public relations administrator, it's important to understand why the news media are vital to school communication efforts—and what the news media want from schools. After all, at one time or another in their careers, many school employees will find themselves dealing directly with the news media.

WHY SCHOOLS USE THE NEWS MEDIA TO COMMUNICATE

Schools frequently turn to the news media to get information out to large numbers of people and when they want to influence what is reported in emerging stories—in other words, to have their point of view reported.

Typically, generating media coverage falls into these broad categories:

- *Accomplishments.* Schools turn to the news media to spread the good word about achievements and successes. They might seek coverage about a new program, a grant awarded to several innovative teachers, graduating students heading off to college in record numbers, state-of-the-art facilities in a new school, and so on.

- *Expertise.* Schools are good sources of expert advice and commentary. And that expertise can become fodder for solid publicity that serves schools as well as the media and the community. A school might offer advice on the best breakfast foods for children heading off to school. Or it might counsel what to teach children about being safe while riding a school bus. Or what types of behaviors to look for as a child develops—and what to do or who to call if you're concerned about developmental issues.

- *Promotion.* Although schools generally are restricted from directly advocating on some issues (voting for a bond issue to build new schools, for example), they often become heavily involved in other types of promotion through news media coverage. *Some examples:* Trying to boost new student enrollment by promoting the importance of enrolling and giving dates and places for enrollment. Discussing the problems that can result when resources tighten—increased class sizes, increased transportation times, higher staff turnover, and so on. Focusing on the growth and opportunity in the district to position it as a great place to work and build a career.

WHAT DO THE MEDIA OFFER SCHOOLS?

What do the media offer schools? *In a word:* credibility.

The "third-party" or "outside" endorsement inherent in positive news coverage can offer a powerful boost to the reputations enjoyed by a school district's schools and programs and the people who run them. But this outside viewpoint can also be a potent tool for eroding public confidence and trust when coverage is negative.

Managed properly, news media coverage can:

- Endorse your schools or programs as centers of service and excellence in serving the community and students with quality education.
- Reinforce your own messages by validating them with third-party, outside reviews and commentary.
- Provide exposure for your key messages efficiently—costing far less and working much faster than other communication efforts used to reach the same audience.

HOW DOES PUBLICITY RELATE TO PR?

It's important to appreciate the role of publicity and media relations in the mix of activities found in school public relations. Why? Too often people associate publicity and "managing" the media as the core function of school public relations efforts.

Some key points:

- Media relations and the publicity that results is only one aspect of public relations programming. It's an important public relations activity, of course, but one that is best used to help reflect and further disseminate the images and information being fostered by communication efforts overall.
- Generating news coverage is not about hype, promotion, or spin. News coverage can certainly be used, at times, to promote activities and ideas, but it does so in an environment where outsiders will ultimately pass judgment on any claims being made.
- There is little that schools can control when it comes to publicity and media relations. The very aspect that fosters credibility of news coverage—the fact that outsiders control the content and timing of messages—means that school staff can exert little control over coverage. But this should be seen as good news. While schools can't—and shouldn't—control the final content and timing, they can and should be active participants in the information sharing and discussion that goes into developing such coverage.

WHO SPEAKS TO THE MEDIA?

Schools have an obligation to work with the news media. They need to be forthright and transparent when communicating what's happening in schools and how the public's investment in schools is being managed.

The media and schools need one another—schools can offer the media an almost inexhaustible source of information and ideas for news coverage. And the media offer schools an efficient way to get information out to large audiences quickly.

So why are some educators uncomfortable when working with the media? Fear is probably the biggest reason. Fear that comments will be misquoted or used in the wrong context to create a negative perception. Or fear that working with or talking with the media is beyond the scope of your responsibilities. Both fears generally are overstated. And they can be addressed with some simple steps.

Some steps:

- For the most part, nearly all employees can be empowered to speak with the media—as long as the context of the discussion is within that person's scope of authority and responsibility. Many school systems have guidelines governing media relations, and all employees should be familiar with them. The specific content of such rules may vary, but the overall intent often is the same. The rules should make clear who can speak to the media and when they can do so. These guidelines aren't meant to be restrictive; they seek to be inclusive and to serve both schools and the news media.

- Guidelines may also govern how media contacts are channeled through the organization. In many cases, such rules suggest that all media contacts should be directed to the public relations department or some other specific office. Here again, the intent is not to be restrictive but, rather, to be service oriented. A central contact might be able to best interpret the request and pass it on to the most qualified person to handle the inquiry. It also recognizes that school administrators and others are busy and often not available to field impromptu calls from the media. This policy also gives administrators a clear way to direct incoming media requests. Example: "I am familiar with that issue, but it's not directly in my area of responsibility. Let me transfer you to Mary Jones in the central office. I'm certain she can connect you with someone who can answer your questions."

- School employees who may have to deal with the news media need to be confident that they can live up to a communications policy that promises open and honest communication. They need to understand that news media coverage will be positive and negative—it covers the good and the not-so-good, but the credibility inherent in this outside viewpoint is what makes media coverage so useful for schools. They also need to appreciate the fact that news media are relentless in pursuing stories. This perpetual process works around the clock— and schools need to be prepared to work with it on that timetable.

- Employees need training to help them understand the rules for dealing with the news media and why such rules exist. Employees can easily misinterpret media guidelines as restrictive, when they are meant to facilitate open and accurate communication. This can result in a scenario such as this: A principal replies to a media inquiry by saying bluntly, "School rules don't let me talk to you. You'll have to call the district office." The reporter might take this as a "brush-off" rather than help to the caller. All school staff members need to understand the tremendous responsibility they take on when representing the school district and working with the news media—it's an important task that is never to be taken on lightly. Everyone needs to understand that the rules governing media relations are driven by a commitment to service, accuracy, and fairness and not by attempts to dampen or shut down communication with the media.

- Finally, training and guidelines can actually help all parties involved grow more comfortable in their media relations roles. Guidelines can help employees better decide when they should not speak with the media—and what to do with an inquiry when they can't respond to it.

They also help employees improve media etiquette by defining the rules for school visits by media, arranging interviews, asking about the scope of a story before an interview, dealing with on-the-spot requests by media who show up in schools unannounced, and so on.

WHAT IS NEWS?

You may not like it, but a sad fact of life is that the events and accomplishments that typify your schools—while vital to you—simply may not be newsworthy at first glance to reporters and editors. But that doesn't mean they can't be used to generate news coverage. It simply means the newsworthy aspects of these efforts need to be made apparent to those who cover the news.

Even if you are working with a school district's public relations office and not directly with the media, helping others see the newsworthy aspects of your potential story is the first step in encouraging the media to cover them. In short, you need to become a newshound of sorts—not just pointing to potential stories but sniffing out the aspects that make them newsworthy.

To begin:

- Pass your potential story through the brutal "who really cares?" test. Forget your own interest in a potential story. Make a list of the story's key points that really matter to reporters, editors, and their audience members. It's not enough to crow that 75 percent of sixth graders improved their math performance. Help others understand *why this matters*—why they should care about this fact.
- Get your facts together and double-check them. The media worry about their own credibility, too, and nothing destroys that more than passing along wrong or incomplete information. Don't share figures, data, or commentary unless you are confident that it's accurate. Over time, the media will become more willing to work with organizations and people whose information has been reliable—and they will avoid working with those whose information is less than perfect.
- Know how the media work. Make sure you understand their needs and deadlines. Reporters and editors on newspapers, broadcasts, and online news sites are filling space and airtime constantly. Reporters working for online news sites may be developing and filing stories almost around the clock. And they will find news to report in that timetable whether or not you're around to assist in the process. *The bottom-line here:* You need to be comfortable working on the news media's timetable, not the school's timetable. This means sharing home and cell phone numbers and e-mail addresses in case

questions come up after "normal" school hours. It also means understanding that there may be times when special efforts may have to be made to meet requests within the deadline of the reporter or editor.

TACTICS FOR GETTING STORIES TO THE MEDIA

Public relations practitioners use a number of tactics to get news and story suggestions to the media. Whether you're using these tactics yourself—or gathering information to be used by your public relations staff to develop these materials—it's important to understand the process and the tools being used.

- The news release is the main item used to communicate news to the media. Short and concise, a news release delivers the essence of a story in about 500 words. If printed, the release is typed double-spaced and rarely runs longer than two pages. It also includes several housekeeping items, such as the date of the release and contact information. Increasingly, the media prefer to have news releases e-mailed to them. Some prefer faxes. In larger school systems and cities, commercial online services may be used to quickly send news release to the media in the region (*examples:* PR Newswire at www.prnewswire.com and Business Wire at www.businesswire.com). Many schools and school districts now make copies of recent news releases available on their Web sites—making them available to both the media and the public.
- Public relations practitioners also use media advisories to alert news outlets to upcoming events that might merit news coverage. Such announcements generally are one page long and contain the basic information about an event—a brief description of what will be happening and who will be present, time and place, special instructions or directions for getting to the site, parking. They also include contact information. Like news releases, media advisories generally are delivered by mail, e-mail, or commercial online news distribution services.
- News can be conveyed in letters (or e-mails if the media prefer). Public relations practitioners sometimes refer to these efforts as "pitch letters," "request-to-cover letters," or "invitation letters." While each may have a slightly different function, they all have the same basic purpose: to introduce a story to a reporter or editor and encourage news coverage of it. Pitch letters often seek coverage of feature stories where interviewing and some in-depth reporting may need to be done. Such a letter, for example, might "pitch" profiles of a few of the outstanding new teachers that have been hired for the new school year. It would include some newsworthy details about incoming

teachers and suggest the kinds of things readers or listeners might find valuable in such a report. Request-to-cover letters might invite a reporter to attend an upcoming event of news value—perhaps a back-to-school training session where a speaker of national prominence might be addressing teachers on current educational issues. An invitation letter is just that—an invitation for a reporter to actually attend an event—perhaps a dinner or some kind of reception. It may or may not be seeking direct coverage of the activity, but keep in mind that anytime the media are included in any event, coverage is a possibility.

- Sometimes a brief e-mail or telephone contact is all that's needed. With a good working relationship and a solid story to offer, a simple e-mail or phone call to reporters and editors might be enough to spark interest in a story. These contacts need to be carefully planned out, with a succinct description of the story ready to be shared, along with contact information for following up. As with all contacts with the media, be sure such contacts are made at the right time. Reporters and editors facing deadlines won't be as open to considering your e-mail or taking your phone call.

BUILDING SOLID RELATIONSHIPS WITH REPORTERS AND EDITORS

Any public relations practitioner will tell you developing good working relationships with all media covering your organization is important to getting your fair share of good news coverage. While media relations activities might be directed by a public relations administrator in some school systems, key school administrators and employees in schools and programs should get to know local media representatives and understand how they work.

Some tips:

- Position yourself as a willing and helpful participant. Be an engaged and passionate representative for your schools or programs. This means answering questions when you can and pointing media inquiries to others who will respond quickly when you can't. *Another suggestion:* Be on the lookout for good story ideas and suggest them when appropriate—even when the stories have no value to your own media relations efforts. You might, for example, hear about a great new neighborhood cleanup program when attending a meeting at your church. If appropriate and the program's leaders are interested, you might suggest the effort as a potential story to a reporter who covers this type of activity. Doing this can position you as a resource to a reporter—and not just another person calling only when you have a story to benefit your own efforts.

- Be available. This may mean offering reporters and editors your home and cell phone numbers—or authorizing the school district's public relations office to let the media contact you in off hours. It also means responding promptly when a reporter leaves a message for you. Even if your reply is letting someone know you are out of town and can't reply, suggest someone who will. Be customer-service savvy when handling media inquiries. Don't leave media requests idling in voice-mail or e-mail inboxes until it's convenient for you to respond.
- Admit when you don't know something, but offer to find an answer or someone who can answer a question. Don't bluff your way through answers or—even worse—refuse to answer questions without offering some type of alternative. Do offer to follow up with information or an answer by a certain time—and then make sure it happens.
- Practice good media etiquette. This means valuing relationships with reporters and editors as they develop, but remembering that these are business relationships. It's fine to get on a first-name basis with reporters covering you and your schools, but ethics rules of school districts and media organizations may frown upon buying lunch or gifts, for example, for media people you work with. Apply good judgment and common sense when it comes to managing these relationships. *Also:* Recognize that media work can be hotly competitive so avoid the appearance of favoring one media outlet over another by sharing story ideas and information with one more often than others. *Other tips:* It can be acceptable to tell a reporter he or she covered a story well—but they generally don't expect or look for compliments or thanks. It's not acceptable to ask to see a story before it's published or to ask a reporter to send you a copy of the story once it is published.

WAYS TO CONNECT SCHOOLS AND THE MEDIA COVERING THEM

Building principals and program administrators can adopt some strategies to develop media relationships before news breaks and reporters descend on schools or offices. *The idea:* Get to know local reporters—and let them get to know you—before a news event breaks. Having a working relationship in place can help to speed up and improve news gathering and reporting when a crisis hits. A school district public relations staff can help to make this happen, too, if that resource is available to you. Even if such assistance is not available, you can consider:

- Introducing yourself to reporters and engaging in discussions to learn about the needs and interests of reporters. Give reporters a tour of the school. Have lunch in a cafeteria.

- Developing a fact sheet or other background information about your school and the people in it. Basic information can be an important resource for reporters trying to get the full story right in the midst of a breaking news event. And it can be an easy way to introduce the school and resources to reporters before news hits. Include key data: number of students and teachers, names of key personnel and their contact information (if appropriate), recent awards or other accomplishments by students and staff, and so on.
- Looking for ways to work with reporters. A reporter might be invited to speak to a class or at special events at the beginning or end of the school year. A principal or others might write an opinion piece for consideration by the local paper or offer to give insight on breaking national education stories that might have local angles. *Also:* Consider letting local media use student work—artwork and writing, for example—as content in the newspapers or online news sites.

SETTING INTERVIEW GROUND RULES

It's always best to work with a school public relations director, if you have one, when contacted by the media for an interview. In any case, it's also always a good idea—and not out of line—to respectfully ask a few questions before agreeing to the session. Your tone should be one of trying to be helpful. The answers to these questions will help you do a better job of supplying the information the reporter needs for a story.

Obviously, you'll want to agree to a time and a place that is convenient for you and meets the reporter's needs, as well. *But to help better prepare for an interview, consider asking:*

- Will the interview be live or taped for later broadcast?
- Who will be asking the questions?
- What are the general topics that will be covered by the questions?
- Will there be others questioned, as well, during this session? In other words, is this a panel or an interview with just me?
- Will questions be taken from callers or persons in an audience?
- How long with the session last?

But what about handling those impromptu interview requests, where you might return to school to find the media sitting in your office? Here again, it's best to ask a few questions before submitting to any on-the-spot interview. Find out what subjects they want to cover and if the interview will be taped for broadcast. It's all right to ask to have an interview postponed, if only for a few hours, to give you some time to prepare. Simply explain that your schedule is full for the moment, but you'd be happy to talk in an hour or two.

CHOOSING A GOOD INTERVIEW LOCATION

Not all interviews need to be done in an office. Picking the right location for an interview is an important consideration if an interview is to be broadcast on television. And many interviews—whether broadcast or not—might benefit from being conducted at the scene of topics being discussed.

If appropriate, consider conducting the interview at a site related to the story. *Examples:* If your story is about a new library, meet there. If it's about a new school, meet in one of the school's classrooms.

KNOW WHAT MAKES FOR A SUCCESSFUL INTERVIEW

One challenge in any interview: Getting the interviewer to focus in on your key points.

Think about the challenge: Interview "sound bites" on radio and television generally run only 10 seconds or less. Even in print interviews, lengthy discussions may be distilled to only a few sentences or paragraphs in print.

This means that you will need to come up with a handful of key messages to stress and repeat throughout any interview, to make sure they come through loud and clear. And you'll want to rehearse the delivery of those key messages beforehand, to make sure your wording is clear—and just as importantly—concise. Time yourself. Make sure you can clearly deliver that key message in less than 10 seconds.

Remember: It's important to get used to the idea that there might be a challenging or confrontational tone to some media interviews. Don't be offended or intimidated when it happens. Reporters and editors also see it as their responsibility to be skeptical of sources.

PREPARING FOR INTERVIEW QUESTIONS YOU'LL FACE

You should never face a media interview without some level of preparation—and you shouldn't feel bad about the need to do it.

Top government and business officials routinely huddle with their public relations advisers to review possible questions and strategize effective answers before media interviews. Giving poor or rambling answers in an interview can result in bad information being reported. Or even worse—bumbling replies can make you and the organization appear to be unprepared to address the issues being reported. Your image and competency—as well as the image and competency of the organization—can be seriously harmed by just one bad interview.

Some simple preparation can boost your confidence and make sure you're ready to deliver the key messages that need to get out there. It's always a good idea to work with others when preparing for media interviews. If your district lacks a public relations staff, other administrators or teachers can offer feedback and suggestions on questions that might be posed and answers that you might deliver.

Some ideas:

- Make a list of all of the questions that you may be asked: the good and the bad. Do this by considering the story you believe the reporter wants to develop. Ask yourself what you, if you were the reporter, would want to ask.
- Write out the overall message that you want to stress during the interview. Think of it this way: If the reporter reports only one message as a result of this interview, what do you want that message to be? Once you've written out your key message, distill it so it can be stated in 10 seconds or less.
- Think about anecdotes, examples, or other supporting information that you can share in support of your key message. Think about—and rehearse—how you might offer these points in support of your key message.

HANDLING TOUGH INTERVIEW QUESTIONS

No matter what kind of ground rules you have set for an interview—or what topics you think are going to be covered—once under way, a media interview is likely to take off in any direction. Just stay calm, listen carefully, and look for ways to bring the conversation back to the key messages you have rehearsed and want to stress.

Some suggestions:

- Be an active listener throughout the entire interview. Avoid the temptation to start thinking about what you'll say while a question is still being asked. Pay careful attention to the entire question. Never assume you know what a reporter is asking before he or she completes a question. Listen to the full question, and be confident that you understand it before answering. If needed, ask the reporter to explain or restate a question.
- Don't fall into the trap of answering hypothetical questions or "what if" questions. Simply say you won't address hypotheticals, but that you will deal with what you know now—then move on to restate one of your key messages. Beyond hypothetical questions, be wary

of directly answering other questions designed to get you to think out loud or offer opinion rather than fact. *Examples:* "How many students do you think will fail if this new test is used?" "School critics accuse you of siding with the mayor's cronies on the school board. How do you respond to them?" "The influx of immigrant families into many of our communities is sure to depress test scores in the future, isn't it?" *Also:* No matter how rough the interview may seem, don't show any anger or defensiveness.

- Look for ways to tie answers to difficult questions to the key messages you want to deliver. Responding to tough questions with replies that link to your key messages helps you to be responsive and to focus the conversation on the story's important points. *Example:* "That's a personnel issue that I can't address directly. *But* what I can tell you is . . . ." *Another:* "We don't have precise data on that issue. *But* there is a significant amount of evidence that shows . . . ." *You might be able to adapt and use these phrases when linking answers to key messages:* "Let me add . . . ," "I'm often asked . . . ," "The most important issue here is . . . ."

- Avoid the temptation to talk too much. Answer a question then stop talking. *Remember:* Your objective is to focus on delivering your key messages in short answers—and nothing more. Don't think you have to say something when there is silence. That kind of unplanned rambling is when interview gaffes often happen.

- Don't assume the reporter is going to eventually ask the questions you want asked. Look for opportunities to offer the answers (key messages) you want to give when responding to the reporter's questions. *Tip:* End your answers with facts or statements that relate directly to one of your key messages.

- Keep the tone of your responses conversational. *Keep in mind:* You're talking with a reporter, not lecturing a class or running a faculty meeting. Your voice and body language also should be positive, enthusiastic, and confident.

LEARN TO LEVERAGE SCHOOL NEWS

Ideas and information that might be fodder for publicity efforts with local news media should be leveraged for additional use in school media as well. And as online and digital communication efforts continue to expand, schools themselves are getting into the news gathering and news reporting business more and more—expanding the options for distributing school news.

Think of this as effectively recycling content and copy that serves an important communication function. It helps to repeat and reinforce key messages appearing in other communication venues. This is how communication programs build effectiveness over time. Don't rely on onetime shots of information to succeed.

Example: A local newspaper might do an interview with a school official on a new discipline code for high school students. This article might be followed up internally with a feature story appearing in the high school's e-newsletter to parents. This story also might be posted on the school system's Web page. Importantly, these follow-up articles, since they are online, can offer direct links to full copies of the new discipline policy for those who'd like more information. They can include "click-through" feedback options, using online forms or e-mail, for readers who want to get more information or ask a question about the story.

Items developed for news coverage might be repackaged or re-reported with new or expanded information for use in:

- School and district print newsletters
- School and district e-newsletters
- School and district Web sites
- Talking points or "factoids" for presentations or speeches made by school officials at school and community gatherings
- Handbooks, calendars, and other annual or single-use school publications
- Alumni or fundraising materials
- Teacher recruitment or other marketing materials

Final tip: Find ways to leverage the impact of the actual news stories appearing in local media as well. Post story clips on school and office bulletin boards. Offer links to the stories on news Web sites from your school Web sites. Reprint the stories on school Web sites (if the media will grant permission to do so). Send the clips to those covered in the story, along with a letter of congratulations.

Q&A: M. Larry Litwin Talks
About Working With the News Media

M. Larry Litwin is a nationally recognized, award-winning educator, public relations counselor, and broadcast journalist who has presented on public relations issues to thousands of students and professionals. Litwin is the author of two books: The Public Relations Practitioner's Playbook *and* The ABCs of Strategic Communication, *a compendium of more than 7,000 terms, tips, and techniques that define the communication professions. Litwin, an associate professor at Rowan University, is an accredited member of the Public Relations Society of America (PRSA) and a member of PRSA's College of Fellows.*

Q: Why should schools care about how they are portrayed in the news media?

A: The news media is an intermediary audience that carries our messages—intended and otherwise.

Perception is reality. As public relations practitioners and counselors, we create, enhance, and sustain our school district's identity. One of our objectives should always be to ensure that our image—the perception the public holds of us—aligns with what our identity should be.

An effective strategic public relations effort that celebrates school and student success will help both the school district and individual schools earn public understanding and support. And remember, support includes financial support as well as moral support.

Q: Is it true that most media simply want to cover controversy and generate headlines that sell? Or are there strategies that can be used to serve both schools and the media?

A: It is no longer true that the media are looking only for "hard" news when it comes to education and other school news. Journalism—print and broadcast—is rapidly transforming from controversy to human interest. It is changing dramatically with the advent of online news platforms and other digital news delivery options.

It has become more the rule rather than the exception to open a newspaper or watch a television newscast and see a major story about a positive school program or accomplishment. Major media organizations are recognizing the value of civic or community journalism and strongly believe a newspaper's survival depends on such people features.

It has become commonplace for those feature stories to drive readers to the Web sites of newspapers and broadcasters. The media recognize that readers and viewers want to know more about the critical issues facing their communities—and school news ranks near the very top.

On the TV side in many markets—large and small—it has become a June "right of passage" for anchors to provide voice-over file footage montages showing a number of graduation ceremonies on successive nights.

Both print and electronic media are concentrating on "town" news that can be summarized in print and on the air and expanded on their respective Web sites.

Q: What are some ways in which school employees should prepare or train before dealing with the media?

A: No school district should allow itself to let more than a few years go by without hiring a media trainer and perhaps a print, TV, or blog reporter to work with small groups or one-on-one with school officials. Knowing how to respond to reporters' questions and appear before a camera takes practice, practice, practice.

While periodic media training is a must even for the best communicators, media rehearsal is, too. When a public relations counselor learns of an impending interview, it is the counselor's job to research the kinds of questions to be asked and rehearse the upcoming session with the prospective interviewee. There is no excuse for not understanding the process and for lack of preparation. Preparation includes having thorough knowledge of the topic at hand, but also how to dress, apply makeup, use facial coding and other mannerisms, and so on. This is where (my) ABCs play a pivotal role:

- Anticipate.
- Be prepared.
- Communicate clearly, concisely, consistently, calculatingly (measured tones), completely (specifically and simply).

Q: When is it appropriate for someone to speak with the media—or should media contacts be limited to only a single spokesperson?

A: Being proactive is the only way. If a school district has something to communicate, take the initiative and contact the media. It could be "hard" news (a major breakthrough, appointment, a resignation, walkout, shooting, or some other tragedy that would be more immediate) or "soft" (feature) news. Among the keys for success:

- School officials must stay ahead of the story.
- If school officials don't talk, someone else will.
- Good reporters will find out, especially if the news is bad.
- Today's "24/7" news cycle means that deadline pressures are greater than ever before.

The use of a single spokesperson depends on the story and the situation. In a breaking story that might fall into the "crisis" category, the research and case studies are clear: There should be a single spokesperson to help to control the message. This does not preclude the spokesperson having a small number of experts—generally no more than five—to assist in addressing the media. Control is the key word when it comes to messages and information so generally a single spokesperson will work best.

If the story falls into the "soft" news or feature category, there might be multiple spokespeople. Those most familiar with it may be interviewed, but official school policy should come from one "voice"—most likely the superintendent or school board president.

For example, retirements—usually announced toward the end of a school year—might include strong feature stories in which the retiree, colleagues, or current and past students might be interviewed. A school might be involved in a major awareness campaign about organ donation, literacy, or families in need during the holidays. These human interest stories need good quotes from a cross section of those most involved with the story. Those newsmakers involved should talk within their own roles or areas of responsibility. But when it comes to school policy, the district's spokesperson should communicate the message.

No matter which route is taken on who speaks, that person (or persons) needs training and rehearsal.

Q: Is "no comment" a good strategy when caught in a sudden demand for an interview?

A: Never, ever say "no comment." Repeat: Never, ever say "no comment." That does not mean you have to comment on everything. There are dozens of ways to say "no comment" without commenting. "No comment" is usually perceived as "guilty" (or hiding something) by the media or at least close to having something to hide.

However, with federal laws such as the Health Insurance Portability and Accountability Act and Family Educational Rights and Privacy Act—and other state and local laws protecting student rights and privacy—it is not always possible to comment on all media questions. Quite simply, respond to a reporter's sensitive questions that cannot be answered by explaining that it would be inappropriate to respond and explain why (in 15 seconds or less) or refer the reporter to an official (not associated with your school or district) who might be able to respond.

If, for example, a crime is committed on school property, the school spokesperson should comment generally—with a strong strategic message—about the health and safety of students and employees. As always, preparation before facing the media is vital.

BOX 17.1

School PR Quick Tips: News Media

- Encourage TV coverage of your events by outlining the visual aspects of them. Good visuals increase the chance of TV coverage. Offer on-camera interview options for those involved with the story. Let the media know if students or teachers, for example, will be available to talk with them.
- Look for ways to link programming and expertise in your school to national stories and trends. These local links can be used to help area media cover national stories with a local point of view—and boost the success of your publicity efforts.
- Enhance the chances of in-depth media coverage of any special event or activity by scheduling it during the "fifth" week of longer months. Why? Many official bodies hold regular meetings—which get news coverage—at regular intervals (such as the first and third Tuesday every month). Few official events take place in the "fifth" week of any month—and the news media may be able to offer more time and space to your event.
- Analyze media content regularly with your school in mind. Keep an eye out for stories similar to ones that your school has to offer as you read local newspapers, watch TV, and listen to the radio. When something matches, call the person who reported it and introduce yourself. Invite the person to visit you and your school. You probably won't get news coverage right away, but you will have established an important contact with someone covering issues important to your efforts—that will most likely pay off in the future.
- Know what makes news. Timeliness is always important. *Example:* A graduation feature is news during graduation—not a month later. Local ties often are essential too. *Example:* Don't talk about national trends. Show how your school exemplifies—or beats—national trends. Humanize the story. Comments by local school leaders or students will always boost the chances that a story will generate coverage. *Examples:* Offer interviews with local science fair winners. Or offer an interview with a teacher who's just presented a paper on an issue of interest locally at a national conference.
- Look for joint-venture opportunities with local media. Can journalism students create regular print or online content for local news media? Can a local reporter be a guest lecturer in some of your classes—and possibly report on the experience? Are any local reporters graduates of your schools—and can they be invited back to do reports on their experience as students and how it influenced their careers?

18

Delivering Your School PR Messages and Content

In Person

Talk to educators about school public relations, and many will point to the stereotypical activities often aligned with such efforts: newsletters, news releases, brochures, and so on. While these efforts certainly play important roles in ongoing efforts to build public understanding and support, they can't do it alone. *Reason:* The quality of day-to-day interactions that all school staff members have with key constituencies (including each other) set the stage for public relations success—or failure.

DEALING WITH OTHERS ONE-ON-ONE

Dealing with people face-to-face is no easy task. It takes planning, practice, and patience. And importantly, it takes a deep appreciation for the *two-way* nature of the personal communication process. *Implication:* Used correctly, personal communication efforts help schools stay connected with their communities and the issues percolating through them. It creates an environment that helps people feel comfortable communicating with schools and an environment in which school officials actively listen to their comments.

When personal communication programs work, problems are identified and averted before they become full-blown controversies or crises. Parents and taxpayers actively encourage people with questions or concerns to deal with school officials directly. Staff members throughout the organization understand and value their roles in student and school success—and use communication to support school activities and initiatives.

The bottom line:

- Public relations planning needs to address efforts to support an ongoing flow of personal two-way communication in schools as well as throughout the school system overall.
- Such efforts should support school employees in effectively delivering key information and messages when communicating with individuals and in front of small and large groups.
- Such efforts also need to help school employees take advantage of the feedback that can be tapped when communicating personally. They need to train school employees in listening actively, responding in nonjudgmental ways, and understanding how to relay information and insights they gather in the school system for additional action.

FACE-TO-FACE TACTICS IN ACTION

Public relations plans work better when they accommodate systematic personal communication tactics. Such efforts become a normal function of the administrative process, seamlessly linking decision making and leadership with the communication activities needed to articulate actions and stimulate support for them.

Some typical tactics:

- **Build a key communicators network.** Key communicator networks can be built around schools or school systems. In essence, they include people who see and talk with others throughout the community and are good sources of insight for school staff members and an efficient tool for delivering critical information quickly—and personally—throughout the community. (For more on key communicator networks, see Chapter 14.)
- **Use informal advisory committees.** Well-formed and properly managed information advisory groups can, in some situations, deliver important streams of feedback and insight to schools. Such groups also can help to signal a school system's commitment to open and ongoing communication. And they can provide important venues for testing messages and information—helping to shape it before it's finalized and released to the community overall. (For more on advisory groups, see Chapter 14.)

- **Make the most of school meetings and presentations.** Every school function—from annual open houses to student play performances—should take full advantage of its public relations potential. How will people be welcomed as they enter the school grounds and building? How well prepared are school employees to run an efficient session—and deliver key school messages? How will event-related communications reinforce key messages and help people understand how the activity is tied to the school system's overall strategic mission?

- **Be a great host.** Look for regular ways to invite outsiders into schools, get central office administrators into schools, and get school employees into central offices. Invite people to breakfast or lunch at schools or in offices. Use suggestion boxes, comment cards, quick questionnaires, feedback forms, and so on—to offer ways for people to share opinions on key school issues at all school gatherings. Encourage support personnel, bus drivers, and others dealing directly with taxpayers daily to track the questions they hear and report suggestions for improving communication on those issues. *In other words:* Always find ways to *ask* people how schools are doing and what is on their minds.

- **See and be seen.** Administrators and other school leaders need to get unglued from their desks and offices on a regular basis and venture out into the community to see and be seen. Get involved in service groups—not just joining but attending meetings, listening to discussions, and taking on leadership tasks. Create speaker bureaus offering school experts to community groups for presentations and speeches. Track local media coverage of school issues, write letters to the editor, or appear on radio and TV talk shows when appropriate.

- **Share good work.** Post videos of important meetings and presentations on school Web sites. Maintain a current calendar of upcoming events online, too. Place PowerPoint presentations and handouts online as well. Have a Web page devoted to key contacts within the school system for those who'd like to be more involved or have an idea or comment to share. Post key student and staff accomplishments in displays in schools and offices—as well as on a special achievement Web site online.

IDEAS FOR CREATING
SUCCESSFUL SCHOOL GATHERINGS

It's easy to think the public relations task has been completed right after parents and others are simply invited to a school for an open house or some other meeting. In fact, the work has just begun. Few people would invite others into their homes without making special preparations—to look their best and make sure people will be welcome. Schools need to do the same to be good hosts.

- Make sure grounds and lobbies are tidy and groomed—creating a good and welcoming first impression. Check signage too to make sure those unfamiliar with the building will know how to get into the building and navigate it once inside. Having people tug on locked doors is no way to welcome guests.
- Find ways to make people feel comfortable. Arrange to have chairs in which they can be comfortable—perhaps using a resource room, small auditorium, faculty lounge, or other area in lieu of squeezing visitors into the small furniture often found in classrooms and cafeterias. Encourage staff to offer assistance when they see visitors who look confused or disoriented. Use student guides whenever possible to help with hosting activities. Students, in fact, should be visible in any gathering—through presentations and samples of their work if they can't be present personally.
- Always plan welcoming and closing remarks that thank people for their involvement and participation and tie the activity under way to key school initiatives and missions. Use the message to help people see the school system's big picture—and how this event fits into that picture.
- Don't let school meetings and events become perfunctory functions where school staff members—and visitors—might just "go through the motions." Have a specific theme and agenda. Tie the event to current issues and initiatives. Make it a celebration of current successes—and not just one more "back-to-school night." *People need to remember:* Even though they may have attended many of these sessions, for many others this is their first one—and perhaps their introduction to your school or school system. Nothing should be routine about any school gathering—each is a new opportunity to display the school system and its students at their best.

PLANNING AND WRITING PRESENTATIONS AND SPEECHES

All school presentations—from major community meetings to small informal gatherings—need to be designed to deliver and reinforce specific, strategic messages and to accomplish specific public relations objectives. While a speaker's delivery at some sessions might be called "informal," no meetings are unimportant enough to get only informal planning when it comes to presentation content.

Another issue: Presentations must deliver key content in a professional, organized fashion. Writing in advance helps speakers organize presentations and economize in words and messages—to not only prepare efficient presentations but to deliver them in ways that *make it clear to the audience that the presenter did in fact prepare.* Disorganized, rambling presentations communicate to audiences that they are unimportant—that their time and needs simply were not important enough for the presenter to spend any time getting ready to communicate with them. Teachers are expected to be prepared before teaching a class. School systems should set the same standard for employees making other kinds of presentations as well.

Some suggestions when writing presentations and speeches:

- **Keep it brief.** It's tough to keep a presentation succinct. It's easy to make it too long and rambling. *One guideline:* Speeches and presentations should rarely run longer than 20 minutes. If subject matter needs more time, then separate presentations and activities need to be prepared to accommodate it. But even a brief, two-minute introduction or welcoming remarks should be prepared. In fact, it's so easy to leave out important information in brief remarks it can be argued that the preparation of a short presentation is more challenging—even for experienced presenters.
- **Use short, simple sentences** and paragraphs with common words people will easily understand. Avoid jargon and abbreviations. Talk to the group about school issues like you might talk to relatives—not other educators.
- **Partner with your audience** by using words such as *we* and *our.* Audiences generally want to see a presenter do well, and they will readily partner with a presenter when invited to do so.
- **Humanize the content of your presentation** with personal accounts, anecdotes, quotes, and other solid examples. Avoid dealing only in numbers and words. Paint pictures for people, so they can visualize your message.
- **Stay on message.** Avoid the temptation to go off topic or ramble extemporaneously. It's easy to burn a lot of time in unplanned diatribes. Good presentations stick to their plan to communicate strategically and reach their public relations objectives.
- **Practice all presentations.** Read them aloud. Videorecord them and watch and critique your performance. Edit content when it's awkward, wordy, and adds little to the effort. Make sure key points are strongly driven home as the presentation unfolds. Make sure it builds to a memorable ending. *Ask yourself:* What key message or two will my audience remember after the presentation is over?

ACCOMMODATING THE AUDIENCE

Understanding any audience—and presenting material in ways that meet their unique interests and needs—will improve the performance of any presentation and the person delivering it.

People want to feel welcome and they want to see themselves as playing a role in any process. A presentation that helps audience members understand how they fit into the issues being discussed—and how they can contribute to success—will build greater audience interest in and enthusiasm for the messages it delivers. This is why school presenters are usually encouraged to talk about "we" and "our" rather than "us" and "my."

Make a list to assess your audience:

- Who exactly makes up the audience?
- What do they already understand about this topic?
- What is their specific interest in this topic—and why are they attending this presentation?
- What interests or activities do audience members share with one another?
- What interests or activities do they share in common with your school or school system?

With your audience outlined, some presenters proceed by creating an outline of key points before actually writing the content. It's a good idea to have a process for the outline as well, to make sure key points are tied appropriately to the audience. Consider the following:

- List all of the key ideas and points the presentation will review.
- List the links between these points—and the links or areas of common interest between the points and the audience.
- List examples or illustrations that can help to personalize or visualize these points for this audience.
- Put the key points and examples in a logical sequence—how the presentation will "tell" this story.

GETTING THE RIGHT INTRODUCTION

The success of a presentation often is predetermined before it ever gets under way. The way in which a presenter—and his or her topic—are introduced will go a long way toward creating credibility for the presenter and the presentation's messages. And it will help to set the audience's expectations—good or bad—for the presentation. *The moral:* Never leave an introduction to chance. Always prepare an introduction for yourself if someone will be introducing you and your presentation.

If there is no formal introduction, *always* take a moment as you begin to introduce yourself and your topic.

Some suggestions:

- Personalize introductions—don't rely on "boilerplate" biographies to do the job. Focus on the part of your professional background or experience that best ties to the audience or the topic being discussed. Be human, too. *Examples:* Note if you have or did have children in local schools—or that you attended local schools. Note if you live nearby, are active in any community groups, and so on.

- Make sure the basics will be right from the beginning: your name is correct and pronounced correctly, your titles and affiliations are accurate, and the title or topic of your presentation is given accurately.
- Try to avoid having those introducing you—despite their good intentions—go too far in singing your praises. Let your background and experiences establish your credibility.
- Once introduced, make a strong beginning. Get under way right away—don't spend time fumbling with note cards or PowerPoint slides before speaking. Let words, voice, and body language communicate—in unison—enthusiasm for your topic and for the event.

CREATING GREAT VISUALS

PowerPoint presentations have become standard for many school presentations. And when used correctly, they can add an important dimension to simple and complex messages. But PowerPoint presentations also need careful development—to make sure they appropriately support the presentation (and don't overshadow it) and to make sure they work toward the presentation's public relations objectives.

But to begin, a presenter might ask these questions: Do I need a PowerPoint presentation to support this effort? Can words alone work? Or can an old-fashioned technology (a chalkboard, a flip chart, a whiteboard) add a low-tech or more human feel that could enhance the presentation's impact? Would a different technology be better? *Example:* A brief video or audio—sharing a solid example.

Some tips for presentation graphics:

- Pay attention to colors, font styles, and font sizes throughout to build consistency in theme and message. Take advantage of slide masters to predetermine fonts, colors, and backgrounds when possible.
- Keep slides simple. Remember that slides function to support presenters, not supplant them. Use only a few words. Make sure illustrations reinforce messages and don't distract from them. Do not use long passages of text.
- Keep the number of slides to a minimum. Audiences lose focus and struggle to keep up when presenters buzz through too many slides.
- Use special effects—if at all—only to emphasize a key point or two. Avoid any temptation to "jazz up" a presentation with special effects—fancy slide transitions, sounds, moving graphics, and so on. For the most part, such devices often work to distract audience members rather than attracting them.

- Don't push your technical prowess or the capabilities of the software and equipment you will be using. It's better to stay in safe, proven ranges when deploying presentation technology. *Bottom line:* Know your limits and work safely within them.
- Always rehearse the presentation with equipment—and a screen—comparable to ones you will be using and in a room comparable to the one you will be presenting in. Make sure slides work well for the size of room and audience you will be facing. Make sure you know what is on each slide—so you will resist the urge to read the slide or speak to the slide when presenting.
- Always have a backup plan in case of disaster. Never create a presentation that depends on technology for its delivery—unless you have a bulletproof plan for proceeding in case the original technology fails for one reason or another.

HANDLING QUESTIONS DURING AND AFTER PRESENTATIONS

Once a presentation concludes, a second presentation often begins—the question-and-answer period. Even informal presentations should allow for time for feedback and audience interaction if at all possible.

Presenters who fail to prepare for potential questions can put an otherwise stellar presentation in jeopardy. One or two tough questions, fumbled at the end of the session, may be what many audience members end up remembering most about the event.

Some presenters prefer to have questions held until the end of a presentation. That's fine in many situations, especially when presenting to large groups. It is important, however, to set the ground rules for questions at the beginning of the presentation so the audience knows the rules. If someone forgets and interrupts with a question, the presenter can redirect by saying simply, "That's a good point and I want to address it. Could you please make sure to ask that again once the question period begins at the end of the presentation?"

But the question period isn't all bad news and stress for presenters. To begin with, most questioners aren't out to "get" the speaker by posing tough or embarrassing questions. Many enjoy using the time to expand their understanding of issues covered in the presentation.

The question period also gives the presenter another opportunity to clarify points made in the presentation, to introduce new points or information, and to reemphasize the presentation's key points.

Body language plays a big role in getting question periods off on a positive note as well. The presenter should maintain a smile and eye contact when asking for questions—and the request should be expressed with some eagerness and in the spirit of opening a dialogue on the presentation. Rather than saying, "Does anyone have any questions?" try "I'd be happy to talk about anything in the presentation in more detail, now. Who has a question for us to start with?"

At this point, there may be no questions. Rather than simply walking offstage looking as if there is no interest in more discussion, a presenter should be prepared with one final point to end the session. Don't just say, "Well, if no one has a question, I guess that's it." Instead, try something such as, "Let me use this time to repeat this important point. . . ." Then thank the audience again for its interest and end the presentation.

Some additional suggestions:

- When tough or confusing questions are asked, avoid answering them until you have formed a key point. There is no problem with simply pausing for a few seconds to think about your response. The silence—if not too long—won't be awkward. If anything, it may help the audience to focus more intently on your response when you begin. You can also gain time, or get some clarification, by restating the question or asking the questioner to restate it or to give an example to illustrate the question.
- Avoid getting into debates with tough questioners. Respond in a positive tone and do so in a way that addresses the crowd overall— and not just the questioner. Question sessions should always be group projects—not one-on-one exchanges between a presenter and a questioner.
- Finally, be careful not to let questioners restate or take over your key points. Example question: "What you're really telling us is that many children are still failing." Reply: "We're dedicated to improving performance by all students—and we're moving on three key steps to make it happen." (Then restate your key points.)
- Know when to end a question session with grace, too. One sign may be that the pace of questions begins to slow—or questions may begin to be similar to ones already asked and answered. Time, too, may become an issue—you simply may need to move on to your next appointment. End a session by simply noting, "We have time for one more question." Answer it, then thank everyone for attending and end the session.

PRESENTING TO UNFRIENDLY AUDIENCES

Most people working in schools will, at one time or another, face the uncomfortable task of talking to unfriendly or angry audiences. Generally, emotions are high. Logic may not drive a great deal of thought. And sometimes even common courtesy can go out the window as those in the audience express their frustration and dissatisfaction.

But dealing with such groups is an essential task. Talking directly to such groups can go a long way to improving understanding and resolving differences. Face-to-face meetings can show that school staff members are listening to concerns and care about reaching consensus.

Some tips:

- Arrive early and try to introduce yourself to as many people in the audiences as you can. Take the chance to shake hands and have as many personal greetings as you can before the meeting gets under way.
- Open your remarks by being cordial and thanking the group to the invitation to talk and listen.
- As you begin, try to acknowledge the group's point of view and recognize the valid points in their stance. Look for ways in which to list areas where you and the group agree.
- Don't engage in boorish behavior—even when the crowd might display it. This means ignoring hecklers. *Why:* Hecklers generally don't represent the crowd overall; often crowd members too are embarrassed by heckling behavior. Avoiding boorish behavior also means resisting the temptation to start shouting over the din of the crowd. If the crowd gets too noisy, try lowering your voice instead of raising it. Exhibit a calmness that others might model.
- Avoid engaging in point-by-point arguments. Such point-counterpoint exchanges often serve to only embolden those who want to argue. Instead, acknowledge and clarify the speaker's main points. Then use the opportunity to review your key messages.
- Make your point and stop talking. *In other words:* Resist the temptation to pontificate, engage in long-winded explanations, or go on and on with complex points of evidence supporting your message. Lengthy answers can further anger the audiences and damage your credibility as people think you're trying to filibuster instead of communicate.
- Take questions—but make sure you understand each question before trying to respond. Listen carefully without interrupting, but ask questions to clarify the inquiry—or ask if the person can give an example of the issue in what is being asked.
- Use comfortable common language people will relate to and understand. Remember, you are not talking to other educators so avoid the jargon that is all too often tossed about in school meetings. Jargon can create the impression that you are trying to hide something or purposely trying to confuse people. So avoid terms such as *resource centers* when you mean *libraries*. Or *food-service facilities* when you mean the *lunchroom. Guideline:* Use common words that will instantly create familiar images (or paint specific pictures) for people.
- Always assume news media are present—even if they aren't. Don't say anything you wouldn't be comfortable reading in tomorrow morning's newspaper. (Your comments may be repeated or paraphrased in letters to the editor even if reporters aren't at the meeting.) If reporters are present, consider speaking with them individually

before and after the session. Offer to answer any questions they might have. Also offer to follow up with more information if they need it.

- If a meeting gets out of control or if you find yourself unprepared for a gathering, apologize and explain you'd like the chance to review the comments you've heard and meet again to discuss them. Commit to follow up and ask a group leader to contact you as soon as convenient to set up a meeting with an appropriate group to continue discussions.

PERSONAL COMMUNICATION DURING CRISES

School systems invest considerable time and resources into crisis planning. Formal plans should address *both* logistics (who does what when a crisis unfolds) *and* communications (who says what to whom when a crisis unfolds). (For more on crisis communication, see Chapter 3.) Such plans need to be reviewed, tested, and revised regularly. A school system's credibility—and the confidence the public places in it—will be tested with every *action* and *comment* made during stressful times when crises—or the threats of them—challenge schools. *Moral:* Even the appearance of confusion or inaction, coupled with a lack of information or comment, can create a significant public relations disaster even when the original crisis is resolved successfully.

What's too often overlooked: the significant personal role every school employee plays during times of crises. Many crisis communication experts warn that the initial phase of any crisis situation will set the stage for the public relations success or failure in managing the crisis. Initial perceptions created among all key audiences will make the difference between a response that is seen as organized and effective and one that is seen as confused and bumbling.

Some ideas for managing your personal communication role when crisis strikes:

- Be familiar with your school system's crisis communication plan and your role in it. Know, too, who official contacts are for the media and other outside organizations so you know how to properly accommodate inquiries that you might not be able to handle yourself. *Remember:* In a time of crisis, parents and others will expect all school representatives to be able to provide insight and information. And in an era of cell phones and text messages, inside "eyewitness" information will be quickly passed on to the community before some in the school system even know all the details. *Result:* Crisis communicators need to focus on collecting information from a variety of sources and communicating as quickly as possible through all media (Web sites, e-mail and text-message blasts, recorded phone messages, the news media, and personal contact by school officials). Understanding how this complex communication will unfold during a crisis is important to school employees—so they can stay informed and personally help others find the information they need.

- Be aware that crises come in many forms. Violence in schools often is associated with crisis communication—perhaps because of the many high-profile incidents that have been given wide media coverage in recent years. But violence in schools is not the only area of potential crisis. Natural disasters (from severe weather to earthquakes and more), health issues (from AIDS to head lice and more), environmental issues (from mold to leaking tank cars and more), and nonviolent crimes (from teacher-student sex revelations to school drinking or drug use, and more) all hold the potential for testing the public relations skills of school staff at all levels.

- Expect attention from the news media and be ready to handle it. Each school system should have a formal media relations policy to help school staff understand and fulfill their roles when responding to the media. But often crisis communication plans call for a single spokesperson or central source of media information when a serious situation unfolds. Many school staff members, however, may be contacted by the media trying to find information quickly, so understanding how to promptly and comfortably handle media inquiries in a time of crisis is essential for all employees.

TAPPING THE PR POWER IN GOOD ETIQUETTE

Personal public relations might be seen as nothing more than using common sense and extending common courtesies. School staff at all levels should always be sensitive to the benefits that can accrue when outsiders see school behavior and responses as courteous and caring.

The starting place: Communicate in ways that make people feel important—showing that they and their concerns matter to you. To do this, little actions often can pay huge public relations dividends. *Some suggestions:*

- Make the time to greet people visiting your school. Introduce yourself and ask if you can help in any way. Remember that outsiders still are intimidated when entering schools and speaking to school officials—even if they don't seem to show it externally. Positioning yourself as being helpful and communicating "as an equal" will create the right first impression.

- Let others see you as someone who holds the needs of others paramount. *How:* Be a proactive communicator—sharing helpful information quickly when you can. Be an active listener—using body language to show that you are listening carefully and incorporating things you've heard in responses. Greet people in a warm and friendly fashion every day. Be sincere when you discuss issues with others—being careful not to be seen as rushed or flippant in any response.

- Always congratulate successes and good deeds. Keep in touch with who's doing what throughout your schools and personally extend your congratulations in person or through personal notes and other means. Showing that you're tuned in to good deeds—big and small—helps others see that you care and their efforts are both noticed and appreciated.

- Make sure you are responsive to concerns and stand out as a model to others on how to handle complaints. Your words and actions should communicate that addressing complaints is important—simply griping and moaning to others about problems is not. Be sensitive to the concerns of others. Make sure you understand them—asking questions to clarify them if needed. Explain what can and cannot be done—and what the steps to finding a resolution will be.

- Admit that being available means much more than simply declaring that you have an "open-door policy." Being available means making the time to meet with and listen to people when they have a need to communicate—not just when your schedule can accommodate them. It includes stopping to listen carefully—and not letting other urgencies create the impression that you are distracted or preoccupied.

- Make yourself visible regularly in school and in the community. It's especially important to be visible with others during tough times—when crisis or controversy may be influencing how people are feeling and what they are talking about. Show concern. Share key information with others. Help them to put issues in the right perspective. Build their confidence that solutions will be found.

- Build partnerships with the language and phrases you use when speaking and writing. Appeal to the self-interest of others by communicating with "you" over "I." Using a "you" approach when speaking and writing will set a cooperative tone that establishes the importance of others in whatever issue you're discussing. It also can suggest that you are more sensitive to the needs and concerns of others. Instead of "*I think this solution will work by helping parents . . . ,*" try using "*You will find this approach will work by helping you. . . .*"

- Using personal communication helps people see and appreciate "the big picture." School systems often spend considerable time developing serious mission or vision statements that many employees never fully incorporate into their daily activities and decision making. Personal conversations with employees, parents, and others can help them to link their roles to the global vision of the school and school system. In schools, good morale and productivity depend on people understanding how their actions contribute to school and student success. Everyday comments and conversations offered by school employees can help others see the fundamental importance of their actions—and create the foundation for school public relations that works.

BOX 18.1

School PR Quick Tips: Communicating Face-to-Face

- Consider getting "old-fashioned" in your communications from time to time to get noticed. A personal letter can be a powerful alternative to an e-mail. Try the occasional greeting card or postcard too for special impact.
- Don't let people play the blame game when problem solving. Getting past blame is essential to finding solutions and creating a comfortable communication environment. Messages need to be communicated that it's OK to admit failure and important to find solutions.
- Communicate that productivity counts. *How:* Make a point to always set end times for meetings as well as start times. At the start of each meeting, remind everyone when it will end. Make it clear that meetings need to be productive and not marathons for indecision.
- Help teachers overcome the "small talk" anxiety of back-to-school night and other school functions by reminding them to ask open-ended questions when talking with others at such gatherings. By asking questions that call for more than a simple reply, conversation will be easier.
- Help people focus on outputs. After a key meeting or training session, ask people to share one idea they'll use to change the way they work when they return to their office or classroom.
- If you rely on a school public relations office for support and counsel, consider yourself a client and behave like a good client. Respect the public relations practitioner's expertise and viewpoints. Engage the office as your public relations partner. Trust their guidance. Respond quickly to their requests—as you would want them to respond quickly to your requests.
- Help staff know how to work with, motivate, and manage volunteers. *Some keys:* Develop formal job descriptions or task lists for volunteers so everyone understands their roles. Talk to people about their interest in volunteering to better understand and appreciate their motivations.
- To better the chances of getting consensus from an audience, consider starting a presentation by setting the stage, then quickly asking for what you want—and then supporting your request. This works better with many audiences than starting with a long list of supporting points and culminating with the formal request.
- When meeting new parents, ask them about their experiences with the school system so far. It shows your concern and may provide some insights into what is working and is not working when people try to communicate with the school system.
- Humanize your communication. Find ways to work people into your language when you communicate. Instead of saying, "The school district found that . . . ," try saying, "Superintendent Jones reported that . . ." or "The high school faculty reported that . . . ." Include anecdotes or firsthand accounts supplied by others in the organization to support key points. Quote and give credit for insights or examples shared by others. *Moral:* Use communication to show how people count in your schools.

19

School PR

How You Can Make a Difference Now

School public relations leader Rich Bagin offers 10 ideas everyone can use. Rich Bagin has worked with hundreds of school districts throughout North America on school communication issues. A veteran of more than 30 years in the school public relations profession, Bagin is executive director of the National School Public Relations Association. He has written and presented extensively on school public relations topics and most recently is the author of the NSPRA book Making Parent Communication Effective & Easy: A Communication Guidebook for Teachers. *Bagin shares his top 10 ideas anyone can use to support school public relations success.*

1. Make the Most of Technology: Web Sites, Blogs, Phone Alerts, and More

New communication technology is adding more and more great new tools for teachers and school leaders. But with it comes with an increased expectation of delivering instant information and results to parents and others. The best programs, however, are never started without training and a communication component of their own. Individual schools and school districts often begin by sitting down with groups of teachers, parents, and principals to talk about these technologies and how they can and should be used. Guidelines and policies should be set so all users understand the expectations and avoid harassing behaviors—like a parent e-mailing three times a day and expecting immediate answers. More and more school districts also are reminding teachers and others about the appropriate and inappropriate use of social networking pages. All school employees need to keep in mind that—to the public—they are the school system, 24/7. Technology can be a major asset to bolster communication and accountability between schools and students and their parents. Effective use of technology also can quickly enhance your professional reputation—while showing that you care about students and about providing access and assistance to help parents and their children be the best that they can be.

2. Be Known for Something

What is it that you want to be known for? A great physics teacher? A well-read scholar and content specialist? A custodian who is proud of the way your school looks? A clerical support person who is known as the "go-to resource" for parents and staff? A teacher who teaches students to think and has high expectations for all children? A school leader who always asks, "What have we done for kids today?"

You will eventually be known for something so it is important to take charge of your own reputation. Step back and assess others with whom you work. What behavior or attributes help or hurt their reputations? Now begin thinking about the steps you need to take to focus on how you want to be known as.

One principal came to be known as "Dr. Frames A. Lot." Whenever a student in his school would win recognition or be mentioned in a newspaper article, he would personally frame the memento and send it home to the student's parents. As hokey as it may seem, this principal helped to build pride in his students and school way beyond the others in his district. And yes, he really was known as "Dr. Frames A. Lot."

School districts can be known for something positive as well. The St. Charles Parish Public Schools in Louisiana give each employee a "Credo Card." It simply states what the district stands for with concise wording:

Our Core Business: Teaching and Learning

Our Focus: Continuous Improvement

Our Commitment: Learning for Life

It also carries the system's mission, vision, and beliefs all contained in a fold-up business-size card. It ends with "Excellence is worth the cost." It leaves no doubt that just about everyone knows what that district stands for.

3. Learn to Write Well, Get Outside Feedback, Develop a Readership, Respect Readers' Time

Always shoot for clear communication. Whether you are speaking or writing, you will persuade more people to pay attention to you if you do not waste anyone's time. Some educators think that they need to impress readers or audience members so they speak or even write in run-on sentences, use multisyllable words, and follow a discourse that leads to nowhere. People respect and trust school leaders who can communicate clear messages with brevity.

To get better, begin by seeking feedback on your writing. Ask colleagues for ways to improve, but also go to a few members of the target audiences you are trying to reach and seek their feedback. See what their "take away" is from what you wrote, and see if it matches what you intended. Revising your writing is a positive attribute practiced by most great writers. So whether it's a memo from the principal on teacher dress codes, a report to the board on new software, or a course on effective teaching, write as clearly as you can. It will be appreciated.

4. Be Proactive

The number one public relations fault of most school employees is that we are not proactive. We are always reacting—which automatically places us in a "catch-up" position. We are always trying to clarify what someone else has said or written about us.

In communication, going first is often the best way to set the agenda. We need to define issues according to our terminology and our timeline and have others react to us. Taking the lead is often critical in the court of public opinion. In recent years, we have seen school districts release negative test scores even before the media can jump all over the less-than-perfect scores. When we release first, we have a chance to position our side of the story explaining what happened and what we plan to do about it.

Learn to communicate and lead by being proactive. It will serve you well throughout your career.

5. Demonstrate That You Care About What You Do and the Students With Whom You Work

One middle school nurse helped a student who sprained his ankle at school and then went the extra step to call his home that evening to see how he was doing. Not knowing of this nurse's action, the school principal also called the student at home and chatted with his parents just to check in about his well-being. Yes, this was an odd coincidence, but it spoke volumes about the culture in that middle school and why parents did all they could to enroll their children there. This same school also had a policy to notify parents when they sensed that their son's or daughter's performance seemed to be slipping. This was not the usual and official pre–report card warning; it was just a caring call or e-mail to alert parents because the teacher cared about their child. Parents loved it because it gave insight on how to help their child before it was too late to do much about it.

6. Let People Get to Know the Real You; Be Visible, Active, and Involved; Join Local Clubs; Start a Key Communicator Program; Make Speeches and Presentations

You can become involved in community and school activities and become a natural advocate and even an ambassador for your school and education in your community. You will be appreciated for your volunteer community efforts, and people will soon realize that your community is lucky to have leading individuals like you in their schools. You can enhance your reputation as a person and a professional by being active with scouting, coaching, evening-class instruction, church groups, or civic associations.

If you choose to get into a leadership role, be as open and visible as possible. Employees tell us that they want to see and hear from their leaders on a regular basis. Staying in touch and showing that you care—with employees, parents, and community leaders—can go a long way in building goodwill as you progress through a career.

7. Keep an Updated List of Five Important Things Everyone Should Know About Your School

School districts around the United States and Canada often print cards with "points of pride"—key facts and data points—about their school districts. It is even more effective to be knowledgeable about the points of pride concerning an individual school's accomplishments or in the program area where you work. Listing items such as successful alumni, merit scholars, percentage of staff with advanced degrees, or school test results is fine. But also think about a storytelling moment of pride where students or staff chipped in to help a student in need, a community cause, or some other good deed.

8. Be Honest and Transparent, Build Trust and Credibility, Reflect Reality, Never Lie or Mislead

It only takes one misstep or "off-the-cuff" remark to ruin a reputation. And once you lose it, you will have a slim chance of getting it back. The Wall of Shame in public relations is full of examples of people who were once at the top of their field and never made their way back. Successful career educators build a foundation of credibility one situation at a time.

Example: While talking to reporters, a school official denies that there was an alleged assault at a school. He describes the event as a minor disturbance that has been resolved. This official had been counseled that such a denial would not be the course to choose—as the school's students and staff knew of the event and local police had been involved. (*Remember:* In today's world, text messaging can spread such a story faster than a prairie fire.) The next day news reports blast this official for downplaying the assault, and include quotes from police, staff, and students at the school. *Moral:* Misleading people is the quick-exit approach to school leadership.

9. Do Unto Others What You Would Want Them to Do to You

For years, I have been preaching that some of the best public relations activities fall into the category of "aggressive common sense." All of us need to look at every situation and put ourselves into the minds of our audiences.

Some bad examples: A parent meeting with 100 people expected and only 50 chairs have been set up; same meeting, the microphone and speaker system do not work; same meeting, the handout is riddled with typos and only 50 were printed; same meeting, the presenter mentions that she is available for questions, and one parent monopolizes 20 minutes with inane questions such that other parents become frustrated and leave.

We need to anticipate and visualize each situation we are planning. What would you expect or be pleased with if you were on the receiving end of your activity, speech, meeting, and so on? Always prepare for situations in parent conferences, open houses, and staff and board meetings. Lack of thinking ahead on how to treat people makes parents and others ponder, "What were they thinking?" And the answer often is, "Well, they were not thinking about us."

10. Be Personally Accountable

Personal accountability is critical for your ultimate success. Always do what you say you will do. And if you can't deliver, let people know why. In essence, public relations deals with building solid, respectful, working relationships with others. When you overpromise or don't deliver, you lose credibility and damage relationships with others. So strive to "underpromise" and "overdeliver."

One way: Take the lead in "closing the loop" in communication. *One example:* If you are at a meeting, jot down a simple grid of the proceedings. For each major item discussed, complete a brief grid with categories of "action taken," "next steps," "deadlines," and "responsibilities." Complete it instantly after the meeting and e-mail it to all participants. Always following up, or "closing the loop," helps to ensure your personal accountability in communication.

School PR Resources

The following resources, textbooks, conferences, and professional organizations may be helpful to your school public relations efforts.

BOOKS AND GUIDES

Making Parent Communication Effective & Easy: A Communication Guidebook for Teachers (NSPRA, www.nspra.org, 301-519-0496)

This easy-to-use guide includes samples and advice to help transform teachers into key communicators for their students, parents, and schools. Written by school public relations veteran and NSPRA executive director Rich Bagin, the book covers a great deal of useful information for teachers: communication tips for teachers, making the most of open houses, making the most of parent-teacher conferences, dealing with difficult parents, and using online grade and planning books. An accompanying CD offers classroom newsletter templates and other samples.

The Crisis Communication Management Manual (NSPRA, www.nspra.org, 301-519-0496)

This step-by-step manual to help school leaders prepare for and navigate crisis communication challenges includes strategies and tactics for reacting to essential common community concerns that must be addressed promptly and properly when a crisis strikes.

Election Success: Proven Strategies for Public Finance Campaigns (NSPRA, www.nspra.org, 301-519-0496)

Increasingly, school communication efforts also include budget and finance communications as well as organizing bond or budget-election campaigns. This guide includes specific planning tips on key finance topics, including setting timelines and deadlines, determining the volunteers you need, creating campaign messages, the role of school staff, board meeting dos and don'ts, proactively dealing with organized opposition, getting the right messages to the right people, cautions about "Rah Rah" campaigns, and dealing with critics of campaign tactics.

Fundraising Tips & Tactics: A Practical Guidebook for Developing New Funds for Special Events and Programs in Your Schools (NSPRA, www.nspra.org, 301-519-0496)

School leaders interested in expanding school services or saving those facing the cutting board can use this step-by-step guide to exploring and implementing proven school fundraising techniques. These are some of the topics featured: how to start a program, targeting prospects, building a budget, linking with businesses, going after foundations, preparing proposals, managing ethical problems, and issues to watch.

How to Say the Right Thing Every Time: Communicating Well With Students, Staff, Parents, and the Public (Corwin, www.corwinpress.com, 800-233-9936) ISBN: 9781412964081

This user-friendly resource, by Robert D. Ramsey, provides practical strategies for improving daily interactions with students, colleagues, parents, and other stakeholders as well as guidelines for avoiding missteps when critical issues arise. The book offers ideas and examples for effective verbal and written communication in a variety of situations—from public speaking and working with the media to straight talk for approaching students about sensitive topics such as sex, gangs, and substance abuse.

Leaders as Communicators and Diplomats (Corwin, www.corwinpress.com, 800-233-9936) ISBN: 9781412949446

This resource offers ideas on effective diplomacy and communication strategies for school leaders. The book includes ideas for improving practice, with contributions from top leadership figures, such as Paul Houston, John R. Hoyle, Rich Bagin, and Daniel Pink. Sample topics: creating a dynamic, effective, districtwide communication system; how superintendents can respond to district challenges and issues; and using blogs as a communication tool.

NSPRA's Scenario Collections (3 volumes) (NSPRA, www.nspra.org, 301-519-0496)

This set covers 63 school public relations case studies exploring the most pressing situations school leaders face. The following information is included in each case study: goals, strategies, and tactics used; successful outcomes; possible approaches; what school communicators would do differently; and contact information of school leaders who faced specific challenges.

Practical PR for Principals: A Handbook to Help You Build Support for Your School (NSPRA, www.nspra.org, 301-519-0496)

This guide offers building principals the essential tools for developing and maintaining a complete communication program for their schools, including more than 100 easy-to-use public relations ideas; fillers and quotes, resources that add instant pizzazz to newsletters and daily bulletins; a sample parent survey; listings and deadlines for national school and student awards to boost your school's reputation; and advice and forms for communicating with parents.

Promoting Your School: Going Beyond PR (Corwin, www.corwinpress.com, 800-233-9936) ISBN: 9781412958134

This book, by Carolyn Warner, coaches educators on how to be articulate advocates for their schools and how to develop the support essential to meet school goals. It includes the following material: information on media relations, crisis management, team building, and parent involvement; coverage of school and community resources to build a support base of human, material, and financial capital; and forms, sample documents, handouts, and checklists for developing a customized school communications program.

School PR Research Primer: Practical Ideas for Getting Data, Driving Decisions, and Empowering Programs (NSPRA, www.nspra.org, 301-519-0496) ISBN: 0875451292

This school communication research primer, by Edward H. Moore, provides needed context and support for using research in school public relations and communication. It provides step-by-step instructions on how to choose the types of research you can conduct and offers ideas on how to conduct inexpensive or free research for your communication efforts.

SCHOOL PR TRAINING AIDS

Unlocking Sensational Service: Tools for Tapping Your People Power (NSPRA, www .nspra.org, 301-519-0496)

This user-friendly CD offers dozens of flexible options for developing and launching a school customer-service program that precisely meets specific needs. Materials can be tailored to create all-day workshops, daily meeting starters, or ongoing training sessions. Sample texts, handouts, discussion outlines, activities, and PowerPoint presentations offer tested school customer-service ideas.

School Communication Workshop Kit (NSPRA, www.nspra.org, 301-519-0496)

This CD-driven resource offers adaptable materials for conducting successful communication workshops for all school employees, including administrators, teachers, and professional and support staff. Materials help participants develop a communication program, identify priority publics, learn to use interpersonal and mass communication techniques, develop a feedback process, and evaluate their communication efforts.

TEXTBOOKS

The School and Community Relations (Allyn & Bacon, http://www.pearsonhighered .com) ISBN: 9780205509065

This text, by Don Bagin, Don Gallagher, and Edward H. Moore, offers a comprehensive look at the theories and tactics guiding school community issues and the communication that shapes them. Chapters are sequenced so students can learn how to establish a public and community relations program that will be effective with all audiences key to school districts and their administrators.

School Public Relations: Building Confidence in Education (NSPRA, www.nspra.org, 301-519-0496)

Providing a thorough look at educational public relations, the text is being used in college and university courses across North America. Its 26 chapters offer insights on subjects vital to building or enhancing a school communication program, from research through planning, implementation, and evaluation. Most chapters are written by practicing school communication administrators.

The SAGE Handbook of Public Relations (SAGE, www.sagepub.com) ISBN: 9781412909549

The SAGE Handbook of Public Relations, by Robert L. Heath, offers a comprehensive examination of public relations practice. It stresses the role that public relations plays when building relationships between organizations, markets, audiences, and their various publics.

Strategic Writing: Multimedia Writing for Public Relations, Advertising and More (Allyn & Bacon, http://www.pearsonhighered.com) ISBN: 9780205591626

Authors Charles Marsh, David Guth, and Bonnie Poovey Short emphasize the strategic, goal-oriented mission of high-quality media and public relations writing with clear, concise instructions for more than 40 types of public relations documents and products. The text includes numerous examples and follows a user-friendly approach, helpful for those new to public relations writing.

Public Relations in Schools (Allyn & Bacon, http://www.pearsonhighered.com) ISBN: 9780131747975

Public Relations in Schools, by Theodore J. Kowalski, provides a comprehensive view of how community relations affect organizational behavior and the effective management of districts and schools. With a focus on communication alternatives in modern technology and political demands for change, it offers an integrated foundation of theory and craft to help practitioners facilitate a positive change in public relations.

Public Relations Online: Lasting Concepts for Changing Media (Sage, www.sagepub.com) ISBN: 9781412914178

This text, by Tom Kelleher, explores effective public relations techniques that can be applied in today's changing, online media environment. The text focuses on how people are using online media to communicate and how new technologies are changing the ways in which people communicate.

PROFESSIONAL ORGANIZATIONS

The National School Public Relations Association (NSPRA, www.nspra.org, 301-519-0496)

NSPRA membership offers networking opportunities and other resources to support school leaders interested in school communication success. Membership categories accommodate school public relations professionals, as well as other educators with school communication roles. NSPRA hosts a variety of professional development activities, offers members a resource-rich Web site, and publishes books and other materials on key school public relations issues. Its Web site also links with an NSPRA research portal in conjunction with the Educational Research Service. (See www.nspra.net for this service.) NSPRA sponsors an annual seminar in June or July.

National Association of Elementary School Principals (NAESP, www.naesp.org, 703-684-3345)

NAESP advocates for and supports elementary and middle school principals and other education leaders in their commitment to student and school success. The organization's newsletter, *Communicator,* addresses school public relations issues and includes an insert, "Report to Parents," with materials in both English and Spanish.

National Association of Secondary School Principals (NASSP, www.principals.org, 703-860-0200)

NASSP serves middle school and high school principals, assistant principals, and aspiring school leaders in the United States and more than 45 other countries. It offers members research-based and peer-tested resources, tools, and materials. Its online communities and knowledge centers offer a number of communication- and public relations–related materials.

The International Association of Business Communicators (IABC, www.iabc.com, 415-544-4700)

IABC serves about 16,000 business communication professionals in more than 70 countries. Its resources and training activities might be helpful for those with significant public relations responsibilities in their organizations. Members generally work in one or more of these areas: public relations/media relations, corporate communications, public affairs, investor relations, government relations, marketing communication, community relations, writing, video production, graphic design, human resources, and public relations teaching. IABC sponsors more than 100 local chapters. It also holds an annual conference in June.

Public Relations Society of America (PRSA, www.prsa.org, 212-460-1400)

PRSA is the world's largest organization for public relations professionals with nearly 32,000 professional and student members. PRSA also has more than 100 local chapters nationwide and 19 Professional Interest Sections—including schools and education. The Public Relations Student Society of America (PRSSA) has nearly 300 chapters at colleges and universities throughout the United States—some of which conduct learning projects on behalf of organizations in their communities, including school systems. PRSA holds an annual conference in October.

WORKSHOPS AND CONFERENCES

The National School Public Relations Association National Seminar (NSPRA, www.nspra.org, 301-519-0496)

This meeting is held annually in July, offering workshops and general sessions on a variety of school communication issues. Sessions are designed for school public relations novices and veterans. Sessions also offer suggestions for non–public relations administrators, including superintendents, principals, and program directors.

PR Power Hours (NSPRA, www.nspra.org, 301-519-0496)

> NSPRA sponsors one-hour online and audio Webinars and teleconferences on important school public relations topics throughout the school year. These low-cost sessions generally feature several national experts. The sessions are designed for use by individuals or small groups of interested educators in a school, district, or region. Topics are updated annually. Recordings of some previous sessions are available on CD.

The Public Relations Society of America International Conference (PRSA, www .prsa.org, 212-460-1400)

> This meeting is generally held in October and includes a number of skill work-shops and major keynote sessions on public relations issues. Some meetings focus on topics of interest to the organizations of many interest sections—including schools and education.

The Public Relations Society of America Special Events (PRSA, www.prsa.org, 212-460-1400)

> PRSA sponsors numerous workshops and online training events on specific pub-lic relations issues throughout the year. Many of its regional chapters and special-interest sections sponsor regular training activities, as well. Current schedules of training activities, as well as links to regional chapters and interest sections, can be found on the organization's Web site.

AWARDS PROGRAMS

Awards programs are important for identifying best practices and recognizing outstanding work by communicators. Such programs also can be sources of samples and good ideas to help aspiring school communicators. All of the major communication organizations (NSPRA, PRSA, and IABC) sponsor national awards programs. In addition, many of their local and regional chapters sponsor awards programs. Information on current awards programs (including listings of winners in recent competition) can be found on the NSPRA (www.nspra.org), PRSA (www.prsa.org), and IABC (www.iabc.com) Web sites.

Index

CORWIN
A SAGE Company

The Corwin logo—a raven striding across an open book—represents the union of courage and learning. Corwin is committed to improving education for all learners by publishing books and other professional development resources for those serving the field of PreK–12 education. By providing practical, hands-on materials, Corwin continues to carry out the promise of its motto: **"Helping Educators Do Their Work Better."**

Made in the USA
Monee, IL
09 July 2020